In Praise of the Open Road

Ababio Ababio weaves a powerful narrative that captures the hopes, dreams and aspirations of many an African immigrant. From the moment his Passport gets the all- powerful-sought- after- and- elusive- magical US Visa, his memoir takes flight.

This story does justice to many similar African journeys into the unknown beyond. Ababio demonstrates that it takes bare knuckle courage and an unshakably determined wanderlust to leave the familiarity of known comfort zones.

Creatively and carefully embroidered into the narrative are the threads of colonialism, post- colonial Kenya as well as the politics and human condition of the now. The unforgiving highly competitive cut throat education system pushes educational immigrants to seek their fortunes beyond their African condition sometimes placing them in direct conflict with their black relatives living out their American dreams or nightmares in the pursuit of happiness.

The inevitable black identity crisis of the African immigrant in America; the ownership of 'blackness' and the myriad of different black experiences from and within the black ethnicities in the diaspora is clearly evident.

Ababio has thoughtfully put together a cast of characters that breathe life into his memoir. From the moment the Americans grant him his visa to Ramji's Indian nuanced Swahili- the tale develops a well-rounded completeness of an African experience- from the root to the fruit. Ababio's poetry is an added bonus.

—Edwin Kegode, (Former teacher of English,
Alliance High School Kikuyu, Jomo Kenyatta High School
Nakuru, St Mary's School Nairobi Kenya) English Department
Meadows School Kent, UK.

'The writing flows nicely and confidently. A very strong message, sensitively yet powerfully conveyed. Great observations of life in the US, particularly small towns."

Kirsten McBride—Editor

"Beautiful memoir, moving and well written. It uncovers issues that have yet in the past been untold."

Anna—Stockholm, Sweden

"It's refreshing to read reflections written by an outsider of American society. For Ababio to write of such taboo issues as intra-race racism shows his American cultural innocence, and to read of these experiences allows me to enter into his world, all while demonstrating his boldness by sharing his thoughts and reactions to the behaviors inflicted upon him."

Sue—Kansas City, KS.

"Carefully and selectively, you've sketched words and thoughts together into this art, breaking the yoke of ignorance. Wisely punctuated with flow and revelation from this cultural duality, is the "Open Road", a book for many readers. It's a thoughtful and flexible gift."

Michael .M—Author of among many others,
"Fear arrests me," from America's best poets
and poems of the Millennium).

The Open Road

An African Walking

ABABIO O. ABABIO

ARPress
ILLUMINATING IDEAS.
EMPOWERING VOICES.

ARPress
45 Dan Road Suite 5
Canton MA 02021

Hotline: 1(888) 821-0229
Fax: 1(508) 545-7580

Ordering Information:
Quantity sales. Special discounts are available on quantity purchases by corporations, associations, and others. For details, contact the publisher at the address above.

Printed in the United States of America.

ISBN-13:   Softcover   979-8-89389-171-3
            eBook   979-8-89389-172-0

Library of Congress Control Number: 2024914625

Dedicated to

Kenyans, Africans, Americans, and people
from the rest of the world who strive each and every day
to break out of tribal, racial and cultural shells.

CONTENTS

Part I
Walking

Part II
Reflections

ACKNOWLEDGMENTS

Thanks to my parents, sisters and brothers for their patience; Late Hon. Henry O. Obwocha for all his support when I needed it most; the late John Mugo, who introduced me to acting and writing. Friends from the past wherever they might be now, including Evans Kanini (journalist), Rose Kuria, and Catherine Wairimu to whom I am forever indebted; Late Lawrence Mukiibi (Uganda) for introducing me to the joys of literature; Zeen M. Zeen (Uganda) for stories on the pleasures of exile and for always telling me, "A luta continua, vitória é certa" (The struggle continues, victory is certain); Tengku Sharizani (Malaysia) for teaching me appreciation of the simple things that life dishes up; Saleh Tayani (Libya), Omar Musameh (Palestine), Kristina Pilhage and Johanna (Sweden), Ed Kremer (United States) for being true friends; to Byron Buckner (United States) for his appreciation of Africa and his insights into the struggles of black America.

Special thanks to Fanta for words of encouragement during the writing of this manuscript. "Africa lives."

Also, thanks to my professors and advisors at Central Missouri State University, Terry Rodenberg, Joy Stevenson, and John Sheets and to Diana Duvall at the International Student center. I owe them the most priceless gift that anybody can offer, and that is a big thank you. Their support, was given to me, full-handed and whole-heartedly.

Finally thank you to my editor Kirsten McBride and to Pola Firestone of BookWorks Publishing for helping to turn my ramblings into consistent and comprehensible musings.

PREFACE

The Open Road is a sojourner's tale. Each day, an immigrant lands on America's shores in search of opportunity. For Africans, coming to America has largely in the past been in search of education followed by a return to the homeland. While on the surface, The Open Road is the author's experiences and firsthand observations, it unfolds complex relationships that face immigrants of African origin as they struggle to get a slice of the American dream. It presents a close look at race, apathy and indifference toward an African immigrant, whose adjustment to a sometimes alien environment is determined by the effects of the colonial culture. To cope, the author develops the ability to glide like a swan between white and black races without being a victim or captive of race. It is a quest that all might not achieve; but one that, despite all the bruises, is worth fighting for.

Ababio O. Ababio.

The Song of the Open Road
Allons! whoever you are come travel with me!
Travelling with me you find what never tires.

The earth never tires,
The earth is rude, silent, and incomprehensible at first, Nature
Is rude and incomprehensible at first,
Be not discouraged, keep on, there are divine things well envelop'd,
I swear to you there are divine things more beautiful than words can tell.

Allons! We must not stop here,
However sweet these laid-up stores, however convenient
This dwelling we cannot remain here,
However shelter'd this port and however calm these
Waters we must not anchor here,
However welcome the hospitality that surrounds us
we are permitted to receive it but a little while.
Walt Whitman

FOREWORD PART I

by Joy Stevenson

In the first part of The Open Road the author shares his hopes and dreams about life at a university in a small town in the Heartland of the United States. He identifies the challenges which he faces and successfully conquers in the United States, but con- fesses the biggest surprise of all is the racial polarization and the lack of connection between African American and international students on campus. As an African student he feels caught in the crossfire and searches for a way to unify and educate the campus about complex cultural issues. His leadership in forging alliances and a new direction for the International Student Organization is detailed and he shares how in finding a new second home and family, he sacrifices part of his Kenyan culture.

After college the author moves to the city as he searches for a professional position, but he shares difficult financial times with other workers. Once he saves enough money to return home to Kenya for a visit, he fulfills his promise to return after ten years. The changes within that time period are startling and he feels he is an alien in his own country where the politics of tribal identification have become dominant. Making a choice between his home country and his new country is very painful, but he returns to his new family of friends from all over the world, individuals sharing a common destiny and dream.

Joy Stevenson, PhD
Director of International Student and Scholar Services
Central Missouri State University, Warrensburg,Missouri.
23 July 2001

PART I

WALKING

1

EMBAKASI

I will wheel from the walls of my home
To the open spaces beyond
The hills, ridges and couched valleys
To the land of unknown.

I will break from the strings of tribe
To the open plains of multiple tongues
Mix and mingle indiscriminately
Like fish in open seas.

I will wing and fly across
The borders of native country
Leaving behind the open sands
The shores and landscape of native land

I will walk with new strangers
Turn them into new friends
Of the new frontiers and territories
New faces, tongues and culture
—Ababio, 1996, By the Shore—

s the sun disappeared toward the horizon, I watched both sorrowful and happy faces surrounding me. Some were happy because I had fulfilled a dream: life could never be the same.

Others were sad, because to my friends I might not be the same when I returned.

"You will come back," a voice from the crowd asked gingerly. "Yes," I replied pushing back tears, "in 10 years I'll be back."

"Remember us."

"I will never forget you."

"Will you write?"

"I promise I will."

Then I turned and boarded the plane. I followed the directions of the flight attendant and took my window seat. For a minute, I had a strange feeling, a mixture of anticipation and fear. As the captain announced the take-off message, I held tight onto my seat. The lady passenger next to me noticed the fear and excitement on my face. I pretended to be confident, stretching my manhood to the utmost. Yet, I felt nervous.

"Traveling for the first time?" she asked. "Yes."

"Where to?"

"The States."

"Which state?"

"Central Missouri State University."

"Hmm, going to college, eh?"

"Yes."

"I hated college."

"Really?"

"Yeah, I dropped out and took a modeling career."

Hmm, I nodded in disbelief, suffering from an ignorance imbibed by our inherited colonial system that trained and produced bureaucrats. To succeed, one had to go college we were told. So, when she informed me that she was successful without having gone to college, I was surprised. But I tried not to show it.

"Want one?" she asked offering a cigarette.

"No, thanks. I don't smoke."

"Good for you." There was a slight pause.

"So where are you headed?" I managed to ask. "New York."

"You're an American?"

4

"Unfortunately."

"You don't seem to be happy about that?"

"Sometimes it is safe not to reveal that to everybody. You know the politics."

"Terrorism is everywhere."

"I know."

She took a long puff and killed the remainder of the cigarette. In the meantime, I glanced through the window. The Pan Am jetliner was churning through the clouds toward West Africa. We were sandwiched between the clouds and huge, tapering mountain rocks that reached for the heavens like homesick angels. For a minute, I realized I had now completely left Kenya and was moving toward a new land. I had high hopes and dreams. I had dropped my desire to become a journalist. I now wanted to be a pharmacist. My parents wanted me to become an M.D. Though it would be a prestigious career, I hated being an M.D. The idea of pricking needles into people's bodies did not intrigue me.

"So what are you going to major in?"

"I beg your pardon."

"What will be your major?"

"Pharmacy."

"Mm, I forgot; you're very smmmmmart."

"I am not smartly dressed if that is what you're hinting."

"I mean up here!"

"You Americans and your English."

"What is your word for 'brainy'?"

"Clever."

"Hmm . . . British, eh?"

"Yeah, Kenya was a former British colony."

"You speak good English though, was it your first language?"

"No, I had to learn it when I was four."

"How many languages do you speak?"

"Three fluently."

"Damn, I just know one."

"American English?"

"You're funny? By the way, how old are you if I may ask?"

5

"Twenty-one," I replied.

"Twenty-one, ambitious, funny." There was a pause.

"So what have you been doing in Nairobi?"

"Vacationing."

"You must be one of the rich movie stars I see on television."

"Nope. I just needed a few weeks off to rewind."

"Did you enjoy it?"

"Can't wait to process the video."

"Where are you based?"

"Milan, Paris and New York."

"Always flying?"

"My surname."

"Coffee or a drink?" the hostess asked.

"A cognac."

"On the rocks?"

"Straight."

"What about you, sir?"

"Coffee," I replied.

"We got cappuccino; single or double shot?"

"Single."

After the flight attendant left, we started enjoying our beverages. Coffee; all these questions; I simply wanted coffee.

"Your folks must be rich or something eh?"

"No," I said.

"Then how can you afford Pharmacy School?"

"Some family friends and the community will chip in the form of Harambee."

"Harambee, what does that mean?"

"Collective effort."

"Must be nice."

"Yes, in Kenya there's that collective effort."

"They don't choose your women for you, do they?"

"Not anymore."

"But they used to?"

"Yeah, but not in our generation."

"Do you have an opinion on that?"

"I will make my own choice."

"True."

She took out a novel and started reading. It was a tour guide for single women traveling abroad. I took a copy of the *Kenyan Weekly Review* and started reading. As each of us got engrossed in our reading, we never noticed the passage of time. Sometimes when she encountered a word she could not comprehend, she sought my help.

"Mtalii what does that mean?"

"Tourist," I answered.

As the night approached, my American fellow passenger looked over at me and asked if I could help her with Swahili. She wanted to surprise her American friends with a new language.

My pleasure, I said. I had found an excuse for keeping the conversation alive.

My eye kept stealing glances at her blonde hair. The effect was enchanting.

"What does your name mean?"

"The Wailer." Hmm. Spell it for me."

"O.T.W.O.R.I."

"Ot-rye."

"O-tuo-ri."

"Sounds musical. I wish I had a name like that." This comment led me to start developing an appreciation for a name that I had hitherto discarded in favor of a Christian name.

"I have always had this romantic illusion of living in an African jungle. In a tent, out in the middle of nowhere," she observed.

I, on the other hand, had the opposite dreams of living in a western world. My Hollywood fantasies began to flower.

New York was 10 hours away. For the next three hours, we went through her travel guidebook. Like an infant learning its first words, she was an enthusiastic learner. But after a while, she flicked off the cabin light and readied herself to sleep. She looked outside and saw the huge moon rolling across the horizon.

"You have a girl friend?" she asked.

"No," I lied fast. "Liar," she exclaimed. "I'm not lying."

"Look at me straight in the eye, liar."

"Not."

"Alright, I give up."

"What about you?"

"Just came out of a bad relationship. The guy was a jerk and an asshole. So I left his ass."

"I am sorry about that," I consoled her. "That is sweet."

"Goodnight."

We finally fell a sleep. Well, I actually didn't. I pretended to. I lifted my leg methodically and accidentally crossed it over hers. She rested her hand across my chest. I pretended not to notice, but my heart began racing and skipping beats. From the adjacent aisle a baby began to cry. Our legs disengaged. Soon I got back in the old position. It warmed me up as the cabin temperature started dropping. We were now at 30,000 feet. Below us, the still Atlantic slept. I tried to suppress my fears, what if we went down, what if? She moved her hand on my chest as she turned. I still pretended I was deeply asleep.

Soon the morning light began to sneak in. I wiped my eyes. The flight attendant was awake, assuring us that all was well. Then she gave us hot towels to wipe our faces. We could see the baby rays of the morning sun. I took the towel and wiped my face. We were an hour from New York. Breakfast was ready. My friend excused herself and went to the bathroom for a make-up routine.

"Coffee or orange juice?" the stewardess asked.

"Coffee no cream."

Meanwhile my friend got back from the bathroom. "Cappuccino, double shot for me," she requested.

She suddenly dived into her purse and extracted a business card.

"Here is my card," she said, handing it to me. I took it and looked at it.

"Is this the last time?" I asked myself as I queued up to get out of the plane. In the meantime I could see her hurry as if she were late for an appointment.

2

PORT OF ENTRY: NEW YORK, 1986

I got off the plane and proceeded to Immigration. There were two lines. One for American citizens and permanent residents, and another for visitors. The latter was longer and slower than the first. Security was tight too. I opened my brief case to remove my passport and a sealed envelope issued by the U.S. Embassy inscribed with the words "to be opened at the port of entry." The contents of the envelope remained a mystery to me. What might they have written? I handed the INS officer the two documents in addition to a copy of my I-20 document.

"Where is the original copy?" the customs officer asked regarding my I-20.

"This is all I have."

"You need the original."

"But that is all I have." I replied, immediately fearing deportation.

"Move this way," he ordered.

Other visitors continued to be cleared. I just stood there, worried. I had fought so hard to get the visa. The previous week I had traveled by Matatu (public service vehicle) from Nakuru to Nairobi to apply for an American visa. I left at six o'clock in the morning and arrived in Nairobi at 7:30. I wore a suit and a tie, as it was almost impossible to be attended to in an official office without being neatly dressed. This was a tradition inherited from the British, our former colonial masters. It was almost like a job interview and I did not want any mistake on my part to cause me to be turned down.

Prior to applying for the visa I had made all the necessary preparations. I had sat for Test of English As a Foreign Language (TOEFL) and passed. I had secured admission at Central Missouri State University based on merit. I had raised the necessary funds to cover my first year. And I had bid farewell to my students at Lake Nakuru High School: the Rugby team, the Drama club and the Hockey team where I was the patron.

I had all my eyes set on achieving the dream of coming to America. If anything were to go wrong, my plans would be put on hold. That would mean going back to my students and trying to secure my job again. It was not an option I was prepared for. So I crossed my fingers and hoped for the best.

I reached the U.S. Embassy compound, where the American

flag was flying high. A couple of uniformed marines guarded the facility. A short, stout one regarded me with the eyes of an eagle surveying its prey. Then he searched me for weapons before letting me proceed toward the waiting area where I picked up the visa application form. I filled it out and took a number, joining the queue to wait for my number to be called.

After a considerable wait, my number was finally called and I was instructed to proceed to window two. "Can I see your documents?" an elderly white lady asked. "Yes, madam," I replied throwing everything to God. Then I handed her five documents: my I-20, my Test of English As a Foreign Language (TOEFL) score slip, a letter from the Ministry of Education, a bank statement and an affidavit of support. She studied the documents once and then again a second time.

"How did you know about the school?"

"From the consulate library."

"Have you any relatives in the States?"

"No."

She matched my A-level subjects with my major, verifying that it was a match. However, she seemed as if bound to find an excuse.

"Do you have your original A-level certificate?"

"No, but I can run and get it," I answered.

"Here, take your documents and come back when you get your original."

"Next," she pronounced and turned away from me to the next in line.

I took the documents and dashed to the Kenya Polytechnic just five minutes away. Since it was Monday, the traffic was heavy. On the way, I kept worrying what if this proved to be a failed trip? I reached the Registrar's office in no time.

"Excuse me, madam."

"Yes, what do you want?" the clerk queried without any sign of politeness.

"It is a matter of urgency. I need an original of my A-level certificate."

"Sorry, he's not seeing people today."

"Why?" I asked desperately.

"He's in a meeting, did you have a prior appointment?"

"No. Please, it is urgent, I need the certificate for my visa."

"You're going to America? Lucky you."

"There's no way I can see him today?"

"No, the earliest is Friday."

In the meantime people were shoved in one after another. Nevertheless, I decided to hang around for a while. It soon turned out that the registrar, who was supposedly out of the office was actually in the adjoining room.

This episode was part of the corrupt system whereby you receive special treatment depending on whom you know. Seeing my disgust, the secretary was embarrassed, as she had thought I was going to leave the place immediately and come back Friday.

"This is my uncle, please let him in," he announced as he suddenly appeared leading an elderly man in. "Where you come from, is it raining?" he continued as he escorted the man to his office and locked the door behind them.

I realized I didn't have a chance, so I took the Friday appointment and headed back to Nakuru. On my way to home, I encountered a guy from my hometown who had been a student at Texas A&M University. I was curious and paid close attention to everything that came out of his mouth about life in the United States. Though he was not talking to me, I made sure that I eavesdropped on the whole conversation. The guy wore a Dallas Cowboys jacket. He was angry with Americans. "Things are bad there," he said to the person next to him, who I later learnt was his uncle.

"Really? That is not what I have seen in the movies."

"Things are bad. Lots of rednecks and bigots."

"I thought black people were rich, like Eddie Murphy and Oprah."

"Those are just a few successful ones. As a matter of fact, I am not going back."

"My son went there, and he has bought himself a car. Are you sure you went to the same America?" another passenger jumped in. "I just want to be a farmer and if one day I see one of those mother fuckers in my country, I swear I'll kill them. I am better here. It is my country. At least I don't have to kiss their ass."

"Watch your mouth, we got children in here," an elderly lady interrupted.

'Watoto siku hizi, hawana hata heshima' (Children these days have no manners).

'Poleni mama, shida za dunia' (I am sorry, troubles of the world) I listened to the whole conversation but decided not to take him seriously. The conversation now had turned from a two-way to everyone in the vehicle jumping in with a comment of some sort. Most stories I had heard about the States were good. I could not allow the words of a one disgruntled person to discourage me in my quest. He might have done something wrong that he didn't want to talk about, gotten busted with drugs or something, working illegally or simply flunked out.

Leaving the States empty-handed was apprehensible.

After all the hype, after all the money wasted how could he face the world?

In no time we were in Nakuru. I got off the Matatu and proceeded home. For the rest of the week, I kept thinking about the things the guy from Texas A&M had said, trying hard not to let them bother me. After all, racism in my country has been replaced by tribalism. I had seen people get higher positions in government depending what tribe they belong to. So to me that kind of thing was the same all over the world. I could not wait for Friday to have my day at the U.S Embassy.

The following Friday I arrived in Nairobi by 8:00 am and headed immediately for the registrar's office. This day I was successful. After getting my certificate I took the sacred thing and proceeded to U.S. Embassy and started the ritual again. First, I was searched and then I proceeded toward the waiting area. Again, I took a number and waited. Finally, I was called this time to window five. I was helped by a young lady with a magnetic smile maybe a recent intern doing her first job. After reviewing my documents, she told me to pay Ksh. 240.00 ($15.00) for the visa. I could not believe how easy it was. She never even asked for the original certificate. I handed her the money and in return I got a visa stamp. I thanked her profusely. I even thought of inviting her to my going- away party but did not know how. She could not have known what an important step in my life this was. My life would never be the same.

My heart had been racing like four-year-old waiting for Christmas. The air was filled with an electric, contagious excitement. My dream of going to the United States was coming true. I felt like shouting and telling my entire neighborhood I was leaving. I felt like punching the air. Later that evening, I was in Nakuru readying myself for the big going-away party.

That was several days ago. Today I am in New York. I watch the customs clearance. They search each person one by one. If you're from Nigeria, the search is even more intense since drug traffickers from Asia have been using that route to pedal drugs to America. I don't have any. After some time, I am cleared. I am in the States. I am in New York en route to Kansas City, Missouri.

3

ACROSS THE PROMISED LAND

After leaving customs I dashed toward the American Airlines terminal to catch my connecting flight to Kansas City. As I reached the check in counter, I presented my ticket. The flight has left, the clerk informed me.

"What?"

"Your flight has just left."

"Well, what do I do? Is there anyone I can talk to?"

"Wait, let me talk to my manager."

After a few minutes, the attendant returned and offered to book me on the next flight via Washington, D.C. That flight was at 1:00 o'clock, two hours away from my previously scheduled departure time. In the meantime, I sauntered around the departure terminal. I entered the duty free airport shop and went through a couple of magazines, *GQ, Ebony, Newsweek, Time* and *The New York Times.*

"Can I help you or something?" the attendant asked, her face something between a sneer and half-smile. It was cold; an aborted smile.

"No thanks, just perusing."

"Let me know when you're ready."

"I will," I replied continuing my free read. Finally, I got myself a copy of *Newsweek.* I took it to the counter to pay for it, struggling to get the correct change.

"You're not from here, are you?" the attendant's smile was now lively.

"Why?"

"You've got an accent; you must be from Jamaica."

"Wrong."

"Africa?"

"Wrong again. No country like that?"

"Sahara."

"That is not a country either."

"I give up. Tell me."

"Kenya."

"Neat, I'd love to go to on a safari in Kenya someday."

"Really, welcome."

As we got engrossed in the conversation, a line started forming. I could hear some black ladies whispering behind me irritated by the fact that the attendant was taking precious time chatting instead of clearing the line.

"Why is he talking to that white bitch? Sell-out," I heard from behind me.

I tried to play it nice and acted like a gentleman. I pretended not to hear a word of what they said. Soon they were attended to and they proceeded toward the concourse.

In the meantime, I played it diplomatically and continued my conversation with the salesclerk realizing that she had heard what the black ladies had said, I switched the conversation.

At 1:00 p.m. on the dot, I left New York for Kansas City. I was lucky to get the window seat so I could view New York from the skies. The Empire State Building, Statue of Liberty and so on. Leaving New York, the plane headed south to Washington, D.C. The stopover was a quick one. From then it was nonstop to Kansas City. I was now flying across the Promised Land. Although I had been anxious to get a good view of the land, sleep was stealing in on me. I submitted accordingly.

By 4.00 p.m. we were in Kansas City International Airport. I picked up my luggage and walked toward a red bus waiting outside. I had been instructed not to take a taxi as they were bound to be expensive, so I felt lucky seeing a bus right away. But I soon realized that the red bus simply kept circling the flight terminal. So, after a while I disembarked.

"Excuse me sir?" I asked a uniformed American Airlines official.

"Yes."

"Please show me where to catch the Greyhound bus."

"Where are you going?"

"Central Missouri State University."

"Where is that?" There was a pause.

Looking at the address on the small map I carried, I said, "Warrensburg."

"Warrensburg? . . . Mm, I'm new here too."

"Ok . . . Thanks anyway." I said. The more I asked, the more confused I became. So, I decided to go at it alone.

I proceeded back to the ticket counter to ask for assistance. Just as I was leaving, a Kansas City metro bus came to a halt right outside the counter. I read the route on the sign at the front: Greyhound bus station. Elated I jumped in dragging my suitcase with me. I walked down the aisle and sat down toward the back not knowing that I was supposed to drop my fare inside the ticket compartment by the driver. How would know? At home, the conductors came for the fare. Finally, the driver instructed me where to drop the fare. We finally reached the Greyhound station. As I was going to get my ticket, I encountered another student returning to school after a summer in Kansas City. From my khaki Kenyan tourist clothes, he suspected I was from Africa. He was a short stocky man, well dressed. "Are you from Africa?" he asked approaching me.

"Yes."

"Where?"

"Kenya."

"Kenya, Jambo, I have some friends from Kenya."

"Oh . . ."

"What about you?"

"Cameroon."

"I see, so do your Kenyan friends live here?"

"No, they live in Warrensburg."

"Warrensburg?" my heart skipped. "That is where I am going."

"Me too. They live at the Kenyan Embassy."

"There's one in Warrensburg?"

"A fake one."

"Well, how long have you been there?"

"Eight months. I arrived in January. I just came to Kansas City for summer work."

"No jobs in Warrensburg?"

"It is a small university town. It is hard to get jobs in the summer. Have you got your ticket yet?"

"Not yet."

"Let me show you where to get one."

Bomba then guided me toward the ticket office. I began to feel a little at home. Here was another African going to the same school. I couldn't hide my excitement. In the bus, Bomba gave me a rendition of life in America. He minced no words. "Life can be hard here, he said. You've got to be willing to do anything to make the mighty dollar. It is hard for people with our skin. But as long as you can work nobody cares." I listened attentively.

"Do you have a car?" I asked.

"Not yet. You don't need one in Warrensburg. It is a small town."

"I have heard so many stories. I had the impression that in America you buy a car after saving for a few months?"

"That is true. For $500.00 you can get a piece of junk with wheels. It can run but not guaranteed."

"Do you know a Kenyan called Sam?"

"Mathenge?"

"Yeah."

"Yes, I know him. Obenge and Tim."

"We grew up together."

"Small world." He stays at the Embassy too."

"Bomba is your last name?"

"Yes, my first name is Fidelis."

"Fidelis Bomba. Mine is Ababio."

"French section of Cameroon or English?"

"English. I speak French, though."

"I'd love to speak some of that too."

"You guys have Swahili."

"That's true." There was a pause. "Are you a Christian?"

"My parents are. What about you?"

"I go to church once in a while."

"Any denomination in particular?"

"Any that opens on Sunday."

"You're funny."

"No, that is the truth," I said.

Soon we were in Warrensburg. When we got out of the bus, Bomba led the way to the Embassy. There I met Tim Kimalel, whose late father had been a Kenyan ambassador to Britain as well as Tim Busienei, Sam Mathenge, Cheptoo Kositany, Mangira and Ed, alias Toro. After the usual greetings we had dinner. I had my first meal in my new country. I was ravenously hungry and almost immediately went for seconds. Tim was a good cook.

"Nyumbani vipi?"(how is home?), Kimalel asked.

"Sawa sawa!"(fine), I replied. "Any newspapers?"

"Yes, plenty."

I opened my bag and extracted several newspapers, the *Daily Nation, Kenya Times, Standard* and the *Weekly Review*. The gang dived into them like hungry dogs. Personally, I wanted to hit the showers and take a nap. Kimalel showed me the facility.

"Where in Kenya do you come from?" he asked.

"Nakuru."

"So, you are a Kikuyu like Sam," Busienei joked. "Kisii."

"Mkisii . . . Eh, so how did you know Sam?"

"I inherited him from my elder brother in Maryland," Sam interrupted. We had become friends growing up in Nakuru. We were classmates with "*Tall*," Sam's brother in high school at The Kenya Polytechnic. He had come to the United States a year earlier. We frequented the same hideouts in Nakuru, Oyster Shell, Pivot, and Gilani's. We are neighborhood buddies.

"You can take your shower now," Kimalel invited.

"Thank you," I said as I walked into the shower. The journey had been long. I stunk. I needed this one.

4

CENTRAL:
THE FIGHTING MULES

The humid summer air hovered over the campus the next day. Being in these new surroundings felt so strange. Everyone was casually dressed. Some girls walking along the pavement wore so little. I could not help but look at them. So, with divided attention, I walked toward the Conference Center for orientation almost stumbling onto the well-manicured flowers.

I entered a room full of foreigners. There were people from China, Europe, Africa and South America. First, we had to take an English test. It struck me as odd to see Europeans taking an English test. I thought they knew English already. Anyway, their proficiency was tested to make sure they could understand American professors.

My essay was entitled "Flight." I wrote it with much enthusiasm. I gave it life as the thoughts flowed without interruption. I described my departure from my native land; the mixed feelings on the faces of those left behind; my first flight. I included my experience at the airport and on and on. The essay scored an "A." I had gained experience in essay writing during my secondary school days. I was one of the top students in literature so I always represented my school in essay competitions sponsored by the various charitable organizations like the Lions and the Rotary clubs.

With an "A" in the essay composition, I got an automatic exemption from taking an extensive course in English. I now proceeded to the registration office. The line was long. The air conditioner was operating at maximum. It was my first encounter with the summer heat. I already had an advisor picked out for me since I didn't know anybody anyway. Later I learned that foreign students ended up getting the hard professors.

"What would you like to start with?" My advisor asked, too busy to introduce himself.

"Chemistry," I replied, unsure of what his question was. "That's your major, isn't it?"

"That is correct."

"You can only take five hours of chemistry this semester. You can pick the rest from Group A: English /Grammar Group B: Oral Communication Group C: Mathematics Group D: Sciences Group E: Humanities Group F: History/Government Group G: Multicultural Studies Group H: Technology and Group I: Individual Development in your student catalog."

I took a few minutes to study the catalog. "Algebra?"

"Sounds good."

"Two more courses."

"Okay,"

"What about philosophy, do you want to try that?"

"Yes."

"Criminal Justice?" what about that one for group F?"

"Fine with me," I said.

"Ok, there you have it." You can go and pickup your printout. In the meantime, take this card. Your next appointment date is on the back."

I took the printout and went to the bookstore to rent books. Then I headed to the residential office to pick a room.

Since I was over 21, I qualified for a room at one of the dormitories, Nickerson. I signed the lease without questions. Being totally new, I thought it was a formality. Later, however, this became a point of contention.

I moved into Nickerson where my first roommate was a Korean, who was on scholarship. Since he spent a lot of time with his girlfriend, I had the room by myself most of the time. Our room was bare compared to all the stuff my American counterparts brought to school. Some needed U-Hauls to move them in. I only made a single trip with one suitcase and a pile of books.

I started my Monday with the math class, followed by chemistry, philosophy and criminal justice. The classes were full on opening day. Later students were weeded out by grades. I soon discovered how obsessed Americans were with grades. If someone was not assured of an A or a B, they could drop the class like a hot potato. I struggled with the classes early on. Although I was much ahead of a standard American freshman, I struggled with multiple- choice questions. In my country, they are rarely used. We were used to extensive essay-type questions. So, I approached them as a novice.

On the first chemistry test, I was so naive that I did not consider using a calculator. These were banned for exams at home. We used log tables instead. As a result, I ended up with a C on the test. On the second test I scored 100. I never again went below that during that semester. However, things were not as good in math, philosophy and criminal justice. I ended up with C's. I wish I had followed my American counterparts and dropped some courses. However, I had this belief that as I settled and familiarized myself with the American education, I'd do better than C's.

I soon noticed a difference in the learning atmosphere in the United States. In Kenya, students participated actively in the discussion. But in some of the classes here when the professor asked a question, it was usually met with stone silence until the professor would say, "That will be an exam item," which would immediately cause a flurry of activity. Even those who had been napping would all of a sudden awaken to highlight the item with their fluorescent yellow markers. Many regular nap takers always took the back rows of the classroom to shield themselves from the line of fire. Another difference I noticed was the habit of chewing on ice cubes during class. In addition, many students, whether winter or summer, always came to class with a mug of coffee or a can of pop.

In my introduction to psychology class the professor, a funny man with a baldhead, kept talking of his roommate, Johnny. Coming from a closed society, I was naïve about rights given to minority groups such as homosexuals. In Kenya, sexual preference is a taboo. Gay people who are referred to as "Shoga," don't declare their sexual orientation openly. So, to me it was surprising to learn that the professor was openly gay. One day when he was discussing sex taboos of primitive cultures in Papua, New Guinea, he made the statement that New Guinea was in Africa.

"Papua, New Guinea is not in Africa", I corrected him.

"Whatever the case is," he continued, ignoring my correction. "The natives believe that fertility comes from the spirit. So when a woman wants to conceive her mate has to kneel in front of his animals and let the beasts urinate on him thus ensuring the transfer of the living spirit. He proceeded laughing at my obvious discomfort.

Everyone now was looking at me like an animal in a zoo. Being an African and the connection of these primitive cultural beliefs, I could not escape being a victim. After all the people of Papua, New Guinea can trace their origin in Africa. Coined with a little ignorance, a misconception can be made.

I was amazed that the professor's knowledge of geography was so shallow. Or was he simply beating on poor Africa like a dead horse? I did not want to keep confronting him with the real facts as the whole class could end up staring at me. Back in high school, we did a lot of research on different countries, especially the United States, the Soviet Union (Russia), and China. I knew everything from the Great Lakes to wine growing in Napa and Modesto Valley, California.

I knew about the Tennessee Valley Authority. I even knew something about steel manufacturing industries. So why was it that in a country with the best facilities in the world, people were ignorant? Maybe it didn't matter. It could be argued that since America is a superpower, there was less need for people to learn about other countries. This is different for a third world child whose success much depends on the policies dictated by these superpowers. They influence leaderships, development loan agencies like the IMF, the World Bank, and UNESCO etc. It is therefore hard for someone of my person to ignore the geography and the policies of such superpowers.

Later that evening, one of the sisters who were in the same class started laughing as she approached me.

"Is anything the matter?" I asked.

"No, just playing with ya."

"So what is Wal-Mart?" I asked after a pause.

"You don't have Wal-Marts over there?"

"No, what is it?"

"You silly dawg, stop tripping."

"Is it something funny?"

"No, it is a store."

"I see. So why was everybody laughing in class?"

"You didn't get the joke?"

"How are ya doing, Kunta?" her boyfriend interrupted, embarrassing me further thereby ruling out any chances of talking to a sister. "Let's go. Leave Kunte alone. Maybe he's thinking about his buddies in the jungle."

They walked toward the cafeteria and left me standing. I was struck by the fact that this was coming from a black student, a basketball player no less. Later I came to learn that the professor was being sarcastic, implying that hair shampoo is readily available at Walmart, an American discount store. He was in some way poking fun at the primitive people and suggesting that they'd rather use shampoo to wash their heads instead of depending on urine from the four-legged beasts.

I was terribly hurt. To add insult to injury, a fellow black brother was poking fun at me and laughing at my discomfort .It would have been easier to take it if it had come from a white but from a brother? I couldn't believe it.

As the days went by, I gradually found out that it was actually easier to get along with white people than with "my own kind." Strange as it may seem. This hurt so much. Some brothers made fun of Africans who bused tables in the cafeteria to make ends meet. I worked at the Union cafeteria as a janitor. I was lucky that I did my work at night, which prevented them from laughing at me. Africans, Chinese, and American whites did most of the cafeteria work. In the meantime, between classes those on athletic scholarships sat there laughing and taking the census of passersby. "Is it kind of hot out there," a brother asked me one day as he took his seat to join his party at one of the cafeteria tables.

"No, it only gets up to 80 degrees and no humidity."

"Hmm . . . then why do y'all guys hate clothes? Like Tarzan or the movie the "Gods Must Be Crazy", is it like that over there?" I was embarrassed. He had chosen this spot to embarrass me. Surrounded by beautiful girls, he had the edge. He tried his best to make me look like a savage animal from the jungle alien to civilization.

"How did you come here, did y'all swim?"

"No, my father owns a boat. I rowed across the Atlantic. Then took a Greyhound from New York," I replied with biting sarcasm.

"Really, sounds prehistoric," he quipped.

I knew I was in for a losing battle. First, I could not understand them; second, they were in a gang and I was the devil on the cross. The sisters who wore their sorority sweatshirts laughed loudly at my discomfort. I was hurting inside. My face reddened.

I knew I was smarter than this ignorant burger. He had not traveled past his hometown of East St. Louis, and yet he behaved like an actor in a theatre of extreme absurdity. Here was a typical misinformed fool. Lack of proper information, or ignorance, has contributed to this kind behavior by people I thought looked much like me.

This kind of betrayal led me to a different approach in dealing with black issues. I felt frustrated as I walked toward my room and swore that one day the brother will realize that despite the material wealth that system provides, he will always be reminded by the system that he is black. I remembered in trying to fit in the system, the black athlete who was trying to run from anything that was African. Africa reminded him of starving children, Africa reminded him of warring villagers, Africa reminded him of a primitive side that no one wanted to be associated with. The more American blacks ran away from me, the closer they were to the western world of material wealth and privilege.

5

IMITATION WHITE

As time went by my relationship with most African American students deteriorated. The closer I seemed to get, the further they drifted away. I tried all avenues in order to belong, but in vain. I tried to learn the slang, but my accent betrayed me. They could always tell I was not from here. Certain unfamiliar words always gave me hard time. On occasions, someone could throw a greeting at me such as, "Wassup, brother?" I didn't know the right answer. I found myself staring at the sky. Sometimes I could pick the last part of a sentence and avoid the pain of having to repeat myself so many times. With a foreign accent, sometimes it was different to pronounce the words the way most Americans did. And unless an American had been out of the country; it was hard for him or her to realize that there was another way of pronouncing an English word.

My efforts to fit into the so-called black culture were unsuccessful. Militant blacks labeled me an "imitation white." This offended me because if there were people I had dreamt to meet, it was black Americans.

But this proved a dream in futility. We shared similar insecurities like lack of acceptance by the racist world. In Kenya, a former British colony, we were under white rule. The European occupied the top, followed by the Indian, and then the African (native) lay at the bottom. Until independence, we went to different schools based on race. I knew my place. Coming to America, an almost white country, I faced the same forms of indifference from those whites who harbored hate for blacks due to ignorance and unfounded fears.

I was determined to reach the blacks and show them that I was affected by the same insecurities that they faced as members of the minority group. To be able to reach them and understand their situation, I decided to become a member of this big association ABC, an acronym for Association of Black Collegiates.

I wanted to join the fraternity, but the pledging scared me. I attended ABC meetings every Thursday in the company of Bobga, even though we ended up sitting at the back alone. Nobody talked to us. We just sat there, listened to the deliberations and after the meeting was over, we left. After going to several meetings, it became clear that we were considered to be strangers and we were unwelcome. In some way, this was my first impression of how selfish some cultures can be. I on the other hand, had grown up in a society where visitors are welcomed with open arms.

However, we were not ready to throw in the towel yet. So at the invitation of one member of the Association of Black Collegiates whose father was an ordained minister of a local black Baptist Church, we decided to attend a church service. I went accompanied by Bobga, as I felt uneasy going alone.

"We have come a long way, people," Reverend Alexander opened the sermon.

"Yes Lord," the crowd roared in agreement.

"We have come across the Promised Land."

"Oh yes, Lord."

"Though there a lot of obstacles on the way."

"Oh Lord, Jesus."

"We shall overcome."

"Amen, amen."

We listened to the whole sermon and after the service we stopped to shake hands with the pastor.

"Where are y'all from?" he asked with a huge, holy smile.

"Africa."

"Thank the Lord, brother, God bless y'all."

We were nicely dressed. Coming from societies where you were treated with respect depending on appearance, we decided to dress well to put to rest the idea that Africa is a backward continent, which has been instilled in the minds of most Americans. We were out to invalidate that premise and prove that in Africa, we are no strangers to clothing. But apart from the pastor, nobody appreciated the effort. I tried to locate the friend who had invited us to church but in vain. Later, rumor had it that we went there to pick up girls.

I did not return to that church again. All my life, I had attended black churches. Perhaps it would be a good idea to try a white church for a change. In any case, does God discriminate between a white and black church? I decided to give a white church a chance. So, the following Sunday I became a member of the First Baptist Church, a predominantly white church near the university.

This immediately raised eyebrows from some black folks. "What are you doing in that white church? a black lady asked me as I walked across to the library after the service.

"Well, I thought they worship the same God," I answered.

"They do, but we've got our own church."

"I have been there already," I defended myself.

"And you didn't like it?"

"No, I was a stranger there."

"You Africans, there's something with you and white people."

"What is that?"

"You guys always think you're better than we are."

"What makes you so sure about that?" I asked curiously.

"All African men I have seen go with ugly, fat white women. Why is that? You just hang around white people too much."

"Is that so? I am new here. This is my first semester."

"You wait and see. You don't like hanging around black people anyway. I got to go."

This reaction early in my first semester was a prelude to what I had to endure throughout my five-year stay in Warrensburg. Such comments were enough to break a person. They made me realize how racially polarized America really was. I was at the crossfire.

Despite this conversation, I went back to the First Baptist Church the following Sunday. Among the mostly white congregation, I saw few Africans and dots of black here and there. Lord knows whether they faced the same ire from their own people as I did. As a member of the church, I got a host family, a young couple from Texas. They invited me on weekends, and we had interesting conversations about Kenya and the United States. The Doyles were interesting people. When they gave me clothes for winter, I was expected to return them after the season or when I got money from home and was able to buy my own. This was an area where our cultures clashed. Instead of borrowing, I assumed they had given me the clothes. Back home, when someone gives you something, you're not expected to return it. It is thought of as a gift.

Nevertheless, once I had a host family, I was comfortable and had a place to hang around on weekends. I was able to overcome my loneliness, which seemed to creep in whenever I thought of home. The Doyles were now family and every Sunday afternoon after the service, I was at their place. We could have lunch together, and then take a stroll along the nearby park. On occasions we could play Frisbee, or touch football. In both sports, I was a novice.

As days went by, I started writing articles for the school newspaper, the *Muleskinner.* Some of the articles were about lack of common social interactions within various student groups. We walked on campus like strangers. African students hang around together; the Asian students on their own; African American Students on their own; white students on their own. I was unhappy with the situation, so I became vocal using the barrel of the pen. Soon, I was at the center of a controversy.

My first confrontation was with some black students, which became heated when I published an article in the *Muleskinner,* entitled "Unity sorely needed among Black *students.*" What follows is the unedited article;

The Editor:
The Muleskinner
Re: Blacks, we've fallen apart

I am writing this letter to address the black students as they celebrate Black History Month. In so doing, I am not trying to act as a referee, but just trying to shed some light on dark spots, which hitherto have been overlooked.

Last week, several speeches were made to kick off black history month. One of these was made by Dr. Stephen Petersen, Vice-president for Student

Affairs. During this time, it could be observed that we blacks have lost the unity of the past. We have created differences between ourselves. We have created rifts, which tend to pull us apart. We are no longer a whole despite the unification by race. We have let the evils of materialism eat into our bonds and hence we have crumbled.

Progress toward a compromise between us has begun to slump and the effects of negative tendencies are beginning to manifest themselves. We now see ourselves in terms of social standing instead of an academic point of view. We discriminate against those poor who cannot fit socially. Where are we heading? Who will lift you when you stumble? Why can't black sororities mix with fellow black collegiates?

A discussion of this phenomenon in no way means we are belittling our identity. We've just forgotten facets of our own advancement. This is my belief that soon, very soon, we will be able to open our eyes and see beyond the small worlds we have created. Then we can be able to utilize the fruits of our academic endeavors, we can, and indeed must, considerably accelerate the pace of our own progress, overcome weak points and difficulties and do away with any signs of stagnation, compose a new hymn of brotherhood. Evolve and bolt out of the shells of ignorance.

In conclusion we are part and parcel of this prestigious institution of higher learning. We have a role to play so we can make the environment better than we found it. Therefore, as black history month rolls on, let us discard our differences and move in the right direction. Note that a critical attitude toward one's own work is an imperative precondition for the success of one's activities. It is my belief that this will not be a pious hope but something based on realistic assessment of our own potential. Then from the rostrum of academic excellence we can stand and face the challenge of a modern human society.

Ababio.
International Student, Kenya

This was a constructive criticism especially coming during Black History Month. In the article, I attacked the split within the black student community. This split was becoming significant. Africans were thought as 'threats." As mentioned, I was always attacked for trying to be white. Leading the charge was Aquilla Butler, a beautiful black girl, cheerleader and later Homecoming Queen runner-up. She said that I was wrong in the article and that I did not understand the black situation. I didn't understand the fact that Warrensburg was a small racist town with a bunch of hill-billies. So why was I blaming the blacks? The system had forced them to adopt the behavior they were exhibiting. Maybe I was wrong. I took time to study and analyze the situation. After all I had been in Warrensburg less than a year. However, sometimes you notice problems faster when you come from outside. I was an outsider and was quick at grasping incidents with the curiosity of a journalist. My mistake was to bring to light something that was hidden within the black community. Despite this reaction from the black community, I got a lot of positive comments from African students and some whites.

"You hit the nail on the head," one Nigerian student commented.

"Is it really like that?" a white classmate asked.

"Don't ask me. This is your country, I am a foreigner. "But I don't have many black friends."

"Why don't you have black friends," I queried naively. "They prefer to stick to their own groups."

"I have noticed that, too."

"You're a different black man."

"How?"

"Your English is clear, and you don't look violent. Is it your first language?" he continued.

"No, I had to learn it."

"Have you ever dated a black girl"?

"No." Pause.

"How do you know I am not violent?"

"I come from a small town and most black guys I've met look mean and violent. If they found you messing around with their girls, they'll kill you."

"Kill you? I thought it was the other way round."

"You're being general, aren't you?"

"At least you guys are different."

After thinking about the situation, I decided to meet Aquilla to try to iron out our differences and misconceptions. We met at Ellis through a good Kenyan friend, Obenge who was residential assistant. Obenge had adjusted well and was as much a black American than an African. He had his hair in a wet Geri curl and was dating a black girl from St. Louis. For me the cost of undergoing all this transformation was not cheap. If the cost of being accepted into the black culture was to try to be "cool," I swore I'd never be accepted. I had to keep my nappy hair.

I was born in Kenya after independence and I'm the first generation independent Kenya. Kenya is a country of mixed races, black and white and a multiplicity of tribes. Being colonized, my parents belong to a totally different generation than mine. Growing up, I wanted to succeed. My point of reference was the immediate colonial master. So I wanted to own the big house, keep a ferocious dog with a sign "mbwa kali,"(ferocious dog). I dreamt of one day becoming a member of the golf club. I wanted to be part of the successful elite. I wanted to study and get an education as a passport to success. My point of reference was not a successful black man because not many blacks were portrayed in a positive light. Instead, the black heroes were depicted in chains. Dedan Kimathi, who fought in the struggle for independence and wore his hair in dreadlocks was not seen much as a hero. Independent Kenya had only changed from being a colonial one in uniform. We had changed guards. We had replaced a white guard with a black one. My image of success was to be part of the privileged or the new propertied class. I had dreams of owning a manicured garden and driving in a Rolls Royce or jaguar like my immediate neighbor. Davidson, a boiler engineer from Britain, had a beautiful home and a green, manicured garden. In a quest to attain this point of reference, I've lost my original purity of being the media creation of a subhuman crook waiting to harm a white tourist. I have lost my pure African culture. So, the environment has largely shaped my behavior. I am not trying to be white; I am only validating the fact that a black man in his environment is an equal to his white counterpart. However, I am still an African, I face the same bottlenecks to success as any other minority group.

At any rate, after my meeting with Aquilla, our misunderstanding was cleared. I pledged to campaign for her in the forthcoming Homecoming Queen election. I cannot hide it; I now admired her and wished we could get something going.

6

AN ELUSIVE AUDIENCE

I waited in vain for black America to welcome or even invite me for a dinner on Thanksgiving Day. Not a single one came forth, but I did get an invitation for a Thanksgiving dinner from one of my chemistry classmates from Devil's Elbow, Missouri. Ed, who is white, extended his invitation without any reservation and even included my roommate, Charles, who was also from Kenya.

It took us almost three hours to get to Devil's Elbow, with Ed driving speedily through hill-billy country. By nightfall we reached town. I met Ed's family and we ate dinner together. I watched Ed play with his dad as he sat swinging on the recliner. Ed drank a beer and joked around with his dad as if they were playmates. The rest of the family was listening to me intensely, wanting to know all about Africa. Later, his mom bade us goodnight as she retired for bed. On the recliner, sleep was slowly stealing in on Ed senior. I had never seen a family this relaxed together. At home, I was used to a serious family discussion at dinnertime, sometimes centering on whether we had done our homework or not. There were no jokes. I wondered if they were like this all the time. If so, how admirable! Though my family never argued in my presence, they were never this loose. Years later after college, Ed got married and I was one of the best men at his wedding. Up to this day, Ed remains a lifelong, true friend.

Most of the black students at Central Missouri were from St. Louis. Some of them had weekend jobs and had to leave every Friday returning late Sunday. Others simply drove off on Friday afternoon after classes to get away from the college town. In this environment, I was wrong in expecting too much social involvement. After all, this was America. This was not Kenya where a stranger is received with open arms. Feeling like a stranger in a strange land, I had to make friends to survive.

Becoming increasingly lonely I started writing letters home and always cherished receiving letters in return. In one of the letters to an old high school sweetheart, I wrote:

Dear Catherine:

It gives great pleasure to write to you once again. In doing so, I rekindle the memories of yesterday; I recall the walks up the hill and the gentle chats. So warm, filled with tremendous anticipation, I was like a four-year old waiting for Xmas. It is almost Christmas here and the weather is cold and snow is all over the ground. I'm sure this is hard for you to understand as you've only seen snow in pictures. It makes me miss home. I've not forgotten you. I hope one day we will have a chance to sling our arms about each other again like drunken buddies staggering home from the neighborhood bar. Won't that be nice? I can't wait.

Sincerely,

Ababio

Around this time all my letters were full of nostalgia and dreams of home. Homesickness formed the only link between my native land and me. I was getting tired of being victimized, especially on the issue of slavery. Was I there any way? To keep my hopes and courage high, I kept writing.

After the first few months, I had not made as many real friends as anticipated. Sometimes I would smile to somebody, but my smile would go an unanswered. Sometimes, a girl would work her lips into something between a sneer and a noncommittal smile. I had thought that in America I could make many new friends. But not a single brother threw me a welcome hand.

In my loneliness, I took refugee in Bob Marley's songs. Bob Marley became a hero because most of his songs identified with Africa. I see another reason why his message resonated. Bob Marley.

In one interview, he mentioned one wish of his that he wanted to fulfill: to reach the black American audience. But it proved an elusive dream. They were not interested in his songs as they thought reggae was jungle music enjoyed by Africans or poor white trash. I found a friend in Bob. Whereas most of the people who were not from Jamaica listened to reggae because of its advocacy of using herb as a sacrament to God, I listened to it for its philosophy and political message. It gave hope to the underdogs and riff raff about their African roots.

I talked to many Africans and other foreigners, who reported experiencing the same coldness. So I was no longer alone. I felt that one reason why most of the brothers were deserting Africans was that the media had shown negative images of Africa such as war, hunger and starvation. Therefore, it was hard for them to associate themselves with us. I was willing and flexible to meet them halfway. However, at no cost was I willing to change my African heritage to gain acceptance by my own kind. I swore to keep my nappy hair instead of getting a Geri curl. I could stay the way I was and still modify my attitude to fit present circumstances. I was willing to modernize my tradition but not to jump into a new culture that I was not sure of.

Some African friends had advised me that to fit into the "cool crowd" by dressing in flashy outfits, playing loud music, one could gain acceptance. This was a tough bargain, a tough concession to make. I had my own pride as an African and was not willing to shed my culture cheaply. My question was and remained, at what cost should I buy into the new culture? It had not yet occurred to me that by trying to pick up the behavior of my black American brothers I could become one of them. I know we are all black in the white world's eye. But the environment has shaped us differently. I sometimes asked myself whether blacks who advocate for having their own state, like the black Muslims, really meant it or knew what they were talking about. Would they survive in Africa, were we to trade places and give them countries trashed by black leaders? Did they know that before independence, we blamed the colonial white rule, yet after they left, black leaders have made some African countries the last home for man? Possibly not. One might demand a return ticket. I don't believe people are ready to take a ship back. However, should an African of my generation be blamed for what happened four hundred years ago? My answer is no. I was not there. Just like we cannot blame young Germans for the Nazi evils, let us not hold a grudge against Africans for slavery. Could it be that the power of bows and arrows could not resist the power of the gun? Maybe. Could it be that a few greedy Africans wanted to surrender their sons and daughters as slaves for export, maybe? However, at this point in history, we have to move on. In the same way it is necessary not to hold level minded white people responsible for what their ancestors have inflicted on my race throughout the centuries.

My efforts to bridge the differences between Africans and black Americans were dwarfed by indifference and apathy. I tried in vain to reach an almost elusive audience. I tried debates, they did not work. I tried writing in the *Muleskinner,* no luck. But in spite of that I did make a few good friends. Most were females who preferred we keep our relationships secret to avoid being laughed at by their friends for dealing with primitive Africans. One of them was Shanne, a nice girl from St. Louis. She was interested in going to Africa some day and asked me all kinds of questions about Africa. After the first semester, Shanne did not come back and when I tried to write to her, I got no reply. After a year, she did come back to campus.

One day while emptying trash at the Union cafeteria, I saw someone familiar-looking pass by in a group of women.

"Ababio," she screamed.

"Shanne," I replied.

"It's been a while, hasn't it?"

"I took a semester off."

"Why?"

"My grades dropped below 2.00, so I had to go rebuild them in a junior college."

"I am glad to see you back. I thought you had disappeared forever."

"That's sweet. I got myself a job in the other cafeteria. Can we meet later?"

"I'm sorry but I am pledging Alpha Kappa Alpha and am not allowed to meet one on one with anybody."

"Oops, sorry about that."

"I saw your name and picture in the paper and want an interview with you for my class."

"About?"

"About Africa."

"Meet me in the office tomorrow. Is lunch time fine with you?"

"Excellent."

She quickly walked away with her sorority sisters who were becoming impatient with her for breaking one of the pledge codes: She was not supposed to associate with anyone outside her sorority.

Amid all these new impressions I was a janitor at night, lab aide and student by day. In addition, I was the International Student Organization president. I ate dinner in the cafeteria, swept and mopped the floors up to 10.00 p.m. I rushed home for a quick shower, then came to the residential library till 1.00 a.m. That was my kind of day.

Somehow, I was able to juggle all these responsibilities. At times people asked me how I managed to work 40 hours and still go to school. "No choice," I answered. Unlike most American students, I was not eligible for a scholarship, Stafford loan or any form of tuition help. I had come to the United States to learn as many aspects of life as possible. As long as I was doing well in my classes, that was fine with me. I was determined to enjoy every moment of my college life, as if it were my last. I found professors accessible. I helped in the laboratory setting equipment for students and graded their work. I worked in the cafeteria and talked with cooks. I painted in the summer. I was a jack-of-all-trades.

This is what I thought learning was. What would I learn if for four years I locked myself up in a library and read all books available? Yet I tried to read as many books as possible. I read Lamming, Naipul, Aime Cesaire, Ngugi, Achebe, Gogol, Chekov, and Tolstoy. I read the poetry of Yeats, Byron, Tennyson, Whitman, Walcott, and Browning. I read to escape from reality. It became my passion. But I always asked myself, why read too much and be labeled a nerd? Life is an adventure. One has to look forward to unknowns ahead, take in stride anything life dishes. Active participation in life is a pleasure that is an integral part of being alive, and that we ourselves can create each and every day.

As a result of this attitude, I swore never to miss any activity as long as it did not interfere with my studies. I attended all organizational meetings and kept abreast of all campus happenings. By involving myself in many activities, I did not realize how time had flown. I started witnessing an evolution of friendships with strangers. I opened myself up to other cultures as much as possible but with caution on certain cultural sensitivities, some of them learnt the hard way. I learnt that for example in some Arab cultures, when greeting someone, a man gives another a very close hug sometimes one could end up stiff not knowing how to react. Such were new things I had to learn. My dream of college was coming true. I was making more friends now than I had time for. I was happy and wanted to keep the show on.

7

MAHOJIANO (THE INTERVIEW)

Later that week, Shanne came to the International Student Center to do the interview. She came prepared. She was formal and business like. After making herself comfortable, she took out a pen and notebook, then started.

Shanne: "Why did you decide to come to the United States?"

Ababio: "In my country, the education system is very competitive. It does not give one a second chance. Once you fail to go to high school, you're doomed. Success is only guaranteed through education. So after failing to get admission to medical school at home, I decided to apply for admission in the U.S. And so, I found myself in Warrensburg."

Shanne: "Why of all places did you choose Central?"

Ababio: "I wanted to get away from the big city. I wanted to get away from the rat race life in New York. Minnesota was too cold. So Central became an obvious choice."

Shanne: "We have our cold spells too, were you aware of that?"

Ababio: "No I wasn't. Like any stranger, I had to cope and adjust."

Shanne: "Mmm . . ."

Ababio: "Strange, isn't it?"

Shanne: "I haven't been to nowhere, so I cannot imagine being so far away from home."

Ababio: "I am used to it now."

Shanne: "How did you afford to come here, are your parents rich or something?"

Ababio: "No, they are just poor provincials."

Shanne: "I beg your pardon?"

Ababio: "They are just average people. Some of my family friends pitched in to see me across."

Shanne: "That is wonderful. I wish we have the same spirit here."

Ababio: "We call it *Harambee*."

Shanne: "Is that in Swahili?"

Ababio: "Yes, and it means pulling together."

Shanne: "I'd like you to teach me some of that. What about your government, does it give scholarships?"

Ababio: "Not to me. You've to be well connected to go that route and I am not. I got a Chinese scholarship to go to Beijing to study pharmacy but having to learn Chinese gave me jitters. So, I decided to come to the States since language was no longer an issue."

Shanne: "How is African life in general? Do you have cities like we do here?"

Ababio: "No, just little huts like they show on television."

Shanne: "You really mean that?"

Ababio: "No, just kidding. We have cities like here. It is hard to tell you unless you see for yourself."

Shanne: "That is my lifetime desire."

Ababio: "Would be nice."

Shanne: "How do you find relations between Africans and black Americans on campus?"

Ababio: "You read the *Muleskinner* article, didn't you?"

Shanne: "You mean to say they are that bad?"

Ababio: "To tell you the truth, someone had to say it and I finally did. Hopefully, it will help open up social and communication channels between the two groups."

Shanne: "I am sad to hear that . . . What about Africans and whites on campus?"

Ababio: "No one knows I am an African until I talk. It is not by choice that my friends happen to be mostly white rather than black. I've opened myself to befriend anyone first as a human being. I am a stranger here, an alien. I came alone, and have no family here. So, my friends are all family."

Shanne: "Can I be family too?"

Ababio: "Yes, yes you can."

Shanne: "You're very intelligent."

Ababio: "My pleasure. Feel free to drop in to the office any time for more information about Africa."

Shanne: "Thank you for the opportunity to interview you for my class project."

Ababio: "Bye."

8

ISO: THE BIRTH OF A LEGEND

The international Club, later called the International Student Organization had its office in the International Center. It consisted of a table and a few chairs as well as mailboxes for the officers of the organization. This office was usually a beehive of activities. During the start of the academic year, all international students had to turn in copies of their F-1 visas and I-20s. Art craft and gifts given to the office by the many international students from almost 65 countries over the years decorated the walls. In this office one could find rarely obtainable literature about the various countries.

Next to this office was the Office of Multicultural Affairs serving the interests of minority students. As you entered this office, one had to wade through a horde of black students hanging and just "chilling." Around lunchtime they frequented the place showing off their various outfits. It looked like a fashion show. They laughed loud and made rude comments especially when Africans passed by, especially if their clothes did not exactly match. This behavior validating the stereotype that blacks were lazy, violent and just wanted everything easy. By any means necessary, I was on a mission to change this.

After several weeks of trying to find an organization to belong to, the International Student Club became my choice. The reasons for joining the club were numerous. First, coming from Kenya, a former British colony, I was eager to learn as much about other cultures as possible. Second, of course I was also ready to learn about the American culture. Third, if I had to learn anything from the white society, joining a black organization was fruitless.

I thought college students had well evolved beyond racial or cultural affiliations, but I was wrong. After several encounters, I realized that there were many groups on campus. Black and White was a big thing on campus; as an African I was caught in the crossfire. So, my desire to join an amorphous organization modeled much like the United Nations was not by a coincidence. I became a full-fledged member of the big Organization. I was a freshman and did not have much experience about the workings of the organization. So, it was with much shock at the very first meeting when elections were held that I found myself in the limelight. I was not prepared for the challenge, but I took the chance. I was ready to be an active member though. I had hopes of one day, may be in my senior year, becoming a president of the organization. So to build my resume, I started from being an active member.

Before coming to America, I had this dream of becoming a diplomat someday, work for UN and maybe someday win the Nobel Prize. These were dreams. Though not guaranteed, they increased the possibility of achievement someday, and so guided my drive. I continued my active participation in the organization throughout the year. I attended all meetings and took time to learn about the organization. Attendance was generally not high. Devotion and dedication were needed.

I was only a sophomore and was not prepared for a leadership role. But it was the end of an academic year and all organizations had to elect new officials. The presidency had to rotate from country to country every year, unless a president was re-elected. A Nigerian and a Kenyan had held the office previously, respectively. During this election, the contestants for the presidency were, Tsang (Hong Kong) and Ade (Nigeria). The members of the organization were mostly African, with a few students from South America. There were few Chinese members as many Chinese students belonged to the powerful Chinese Student Organization, which was almost a political party.

The idea of an international club meant that the organization should have an international flavor reflecting diversity. The fact that the president had been an African twice recently gave it an African outlook. We had to change this, as it was intimidating to students from Europe, China, India, and Malaysia who wanted their share of the presidency. So when Tsang declared his intention to run, we decided to support him instead of the other African student. This did not go well with Ade (Nigeria), who accused the Kenyans of selling out. Ade had thought that since there were so many African countries in the organization, he could easily win. He counted in his column, Nigeria, Cameroon, Ghana, Zambia, Ethiopia, Liberia, Sierra Leone, Libya and Kenya. Surprisingly, Kenya, Libya, Palestine, Chile, Hong Hong, China, Taiwan (ROC), Korea, Sweden, England voted for Tsang (Hong Kong) who won the vote. I was elected vice-president despite opposition from Ade, who refused to take defeat lightly. Lee (Korea) was social coordinator, Kim Kam (Malaysia) became treasurer and Cha Lin Meng (Taiwan) took the role of secretary. There was some diversity now, though Asia was in total control.

As Dr. Joy Stevenson, the international students advisor, announced the results, there was a lot of mumbling. "They have given it to the Orientals," some said.

I decided to stick with the Kenyan decision. As time went by,

the Nigeria delegation dropped out of meetings. Cameroon soon followed. At our first meeting, only Kenya and Libya represented Africa. So here I was representing not only Kenya, but also the entire African continent. Asia had a large delegation led by China, Korea, Malaysia, Taiwan, and Hong Kong. We were at least assured of support from the influential

Chinese Student Association (CSA). This association operated with the secrecy of the communist party. They met Chinese students on arrival and recruited them. They then inoculated them against using English on campus for some reason I did not understand. I never bothered to ask.

"So why did they quit?" Tsang asked me one day.

"I do not know. I guess they took defeat painfully," I answered.

"It is supposed to be fun, isn't it?"

"That is my belief."

"Can you do me a favor?"

"What?"

"I want to call a general meeting on Sunday."

"Sunday, that is only two days away."

"Yes, I decided that since Dr. Joy was sending out mail to all international students, I decided to add the announcement for the meeting."

"I see, that is fine."

"So, I'll appreciate if you drop off most of the mail to Greenwood Park."

"Fine with me."

I took the letters to Greenwood Park, a residential trailer park for married students. A lot of African students who had families lived here. Among them, Ade. I drove there in my big beige Pontiac Catalina, given to me for free by Hakim, a friend from Libya. I reached the park in five minutes and I was about to paste up the letter on to the trailer park door, when the door suddenly flew open.

"Come in, have a seat," Ade invited.

"I am in a hurr y; I still have a lot to deliver," I said uncomfortably.

"Where are they from, Joy Stevenson?"

"No, it is from the club."

"So you Kenyans are like that, eh?"

"It was a group decision. I had no control over it."

"Group thing, eh." Well, I have no time for the club. I am too busy with school work."

"I thought you were still interested in the presidency next year, aren't you?"

"You Kenyans are just hypocrites."

"We didn't hide anything, Ade."

"You guys have the organization with the Orientals."

He ripped the letter in shreds without even reading it. I walked away and delivered the rest.

At 6 o'clock that Sunday, Tsang sat looking at his watch to validate the time on the wall. There were three other officials and I. We had expected 30 people. By 6:30, we could not wait any longer. Tsang was under extreme pressure. It was not the kind of start one expects on taking the presidency. Tsang had planned an aggressive agenda including visits to various international clubs in other universities to see how they conducted cultural events. As it turned out, on this Sunday meeting top of the agenda was a trip to Rolla to attend an international cultural night. Being a week away, a decision had to be reached to enable the treasurer to request funding from the student financial board.

Without wasting much time, Tsang presided over the meeting in which the Rolla trip was discussed and approved without much deliberation. The other items on the agenda were on how to improve student participation in the club. As time went by though, galvanizing international students was not as easy and gradually Tsang felt betrayed by lack of enthusiasm and lackadaisical participation in club activities. He also hinted of transferring to another school, which offered him a better stipend. His credentials were impressive having graduated from Washington University in St. Louis. He was a very smart guy. When he was my roommate, he read the whole night. Sometimes he would go to sleep early and then wake up in the middle of the night and stagger to his office to read to avoid driving me nuts with the light.

By the end of the semester, Tsang was out of CMSU. We were now faced with two choices. One, call for election, or two, for me to step in as president. I went to Dr. Joy Stevenson's office and consulted with her. She asked whether I was interested in taking the challenge. Being only a sophomore, I was nervous. I had only been vice president for one semester. Truthfully, I was nervous about taking the job but decided to give it a try.

My first mission was to see that the International Club reclaimed not only international flavor but also diversity. One way to do this was to seek recommendations and use the power of my office to make executive appointments. First on board was Saleh Tayani, from Libya, who became vice-president. My friend Hakim, who had been a member of the club, recommended him. Next came Kim Kam from Malaysia as treasurer. With Saleh, the Muslim Students Association was on board while Kim brought Malaysia with her. I retained the other officers.

My next mission was to have an audience with presidents of other foreign organizations like the Chinese Students Association, the Hong Kong Students Association, the Malaysian Students Association, the Thai Students Association and the Kenyan Students Association. All pledged to participate in an international cultural night that I proposed.

To plan the event, I had a meeting with some Malaysian students and in came Tengku Zaharizan, prophetic-looking Malay. Tengku had been a stage director in Malaysia, so he ended up as production manager. After we started soliciting entries for the show, Malaysia was first to submit an entry. Cameroon submitted an entry through their lone ambassador, Bobga. Other entries came from Kenya, China, Taiwan, the Muslim Students Association and Ghana. To represent America, I asked a friend of mine to get someone to sing the national anthem. She could not wait to do it. So bingo, we were ready to go.

Then came the day of the show. The union hall was set up to accommodate 200 people. We had hoped to get 50. After all, it was our first show. By 6:30 p.m. 150 people had gone through the food line. Our audience was mixed: children, faculty and staff as well as people from the local community. Unfortunately, it lacked a lot of American students, an audience we had hoped to capture. Chances are they had left for home on Friday as usual.

The evening started with Tonya singing the national anthem. Then came the Malaysians with a Pink Floyd type of rendition, Razaza . . . heri . . . raza a Malay folk song. Then came the Kenyan celebration dance (sukuti), followed by a Chinese dance, a Thai dance, a Hong Kong dragon show and so on. The evening concluded with a fashion show. The audience stayed with us to the end. We knew we had captured some hearts. We could not wait for the next event.

As I sat later that evening in my room, a lot of congratulatory messages came in. The next morning Dr. Joy Stevenson's face lit up. She was thrilled and flattered to be the head of such a successful organization. We had created anticipation for the first time. As time went by, new members started joining the organization. Every foreign student in the school wanted to be part of it. When it was time for elections at the end of the semester, the race for presidency had suddenly become competitive. To be elected to office, one had to be an active member.

Since I had not been officially elected president, I decided to run on my own terms with my present team to get a mandate from the members. We ran as a team with all the incumbent officials who decided to serve another term. Apart from the presidency, the other office holders were eligible for reelection. These people had sacrificed their time to attend meetings and Club activities. To reward them, I felt they needed to be elected and maintain continuity in the Organization. The team included, Saleh Tayani, Kim Kam, Bernard Chang, Cha Lin Meng, Lynda Koo, Tengku and Luis Cedeno. The ticket won.

After the elections we held a press conference and announced the new executive board. In an effort to reach out to all the other diverse student groups on campus, I appointed a representative to the Association of Black Collegiates, Student Government Association and other organizations of interest. Finally, we enlisted a permanent reporter from the *Muleskinner* to cover our events. ISO was a visible organization on campus. Finally, my dream of being part of the big organization was coming true.

9

AMERICANS, ISO IS FOR YOU TOO

People of the world
All races, tribes and cultures
You only need to sing
Peace one world
Allons, thy light has come.
Ababio©1989 *(Muleskinner, November 30,1989)*

I t was our desire to take ISO to the community. To do so, we had to make the organization accessible to students, community members, children, faculty and staff. In this way, we could change our image and make the organization unique. If fraternities and sororities catered to special interest groups on campus, we had to cater for a wide variety group. So the focus of our programs was much to the taste of the community.

We reduced the number of parties to one per semester and made sure that fund-raising events came at the end of a cultural festival. We had to do this to avoid the negative image that had been cast by some organizations on campus. They had become hotbeds of violence caused by excessive partying and use of alcohol.

So, to avoid being on the same category, we structured our activities accordingly. In doing this we could keep our audience of community members, children and families. We were sensitive to all cultures and tried to avoid offending anybody. Cultural diversity was the springboard of our organization, and it was from this amalgam that all of us could draw. We paid tribute to America by singing the national anthem before any of our cultural activities. That year, an American student and former beauty queen sang the anthem. In a matter of symbolism, we had six countries on stage to form a circle to represent five continents plus America. We tried to be as creative as possible.

In scheduling events, we planned to have an activity either after spring break or after Thanksgiving break so as to trap as many students as possible. Also, our members would be less busy immediately after any break and therefore have more time to work on the event.

In November 18, 1989, ISO presented a Peace One-World Cultural Festival to commemorate its tenth-year anniversary. This was the climax of the year with an attendance of 600. This was followed April 8 with an event headlined in the *Muleskinner* as *"Dances, traditions highlight evening."* The reported attendance was 450, with 39 countries represented.

It was a time for me to extend my hand once again, so we had invited the black collegiates to be part of the show. "Come . . . come and be part of the world stage," I told them. You don't need to run away. It is peace, one world." I had won them over finally, I thought. The cultural night exceeded our expectations. We had managed to unite the school community. Everyone was proud of being a part of ISO. We had opened it to everyone. Other organizations envied our collectiveness. In this community, I had found a second home. I had seen how ISO had managed to cut through diverse cultural backgrounds.

I was entering my senior year the following year. I was under pressure to perform in class as well as in the open arena. Behind the scenes, I worked 20 hours in the lab plus 20 hours in the cafeteria. Yet nobody knew my life offstage. I received no money from home, but through my active participation in ISO securing short-term loans for tuition had become easier. I maintained my smile and waded through the multiple cultures.

Later that semester, Saleh succeeded me as president. Kim retired. My public life throughout my tenure as president had become so visible. It was hard to keep a steady relationship because I was always on center stage. I wanted time off. My public life needed editing.

10

AFRICA RISE, THY LIGHT HAS COME

It is morning Africa
And hope is within grasp Give me the power to say Africa rise,
thy light has come.
Ababio©1990 All Rights Reserved

After my two-term tenure as ISO president, it was time to take a low profile and enjoy a little private life. But another responsibility soon presented itself. A group of African students thought it wise to form an African organization to serve their interests and collectively solve problems affecting them individually. I offered to help draft the constitution. After the constitution work was done, I received numerous requests to lead the infant organization, in the hope that the organization would grow in the mould of ISO. At the same time, the Kenyan Student Association (KSA) requested me to be an official in their organization. It was a hard decision to make being a Kenyan. I weighed the two options and agreed to serve on a less demanding role of being the editor of their annual newsletter, *"Mwananchi"*.

Meanwhile, I accepted the nomination for president of the Organization of African Students (OAS). At the member meeting two weeks later, I was elected president.

To give the organization a continental outlook, Joseph Okoduwa (Nigeria) became vice president, Evans Amatoru (Nigeria) financial secretary, Mary Ngotho (Kenya) secretary general, Barnabas Azike (Nigeria) public relations officer, Pauline Cheruyoit (Kenya) treasurer, Fanson Kidwaro (Kenya) speaker of the house, Cletus Titalangha (Cameroon) delegate, Saleh Tayani (Libya) delegate, and Simon Oladimeji (Nigeria), editor of *Africana,* OAS mouthpiece.

After the election we decided to open the organization to all students on campus who were interested in an African organization. This made it easier to interact with all the students and to reach out to an audience that had proved elusive. To take the ball to the court of black Americans, we decided to dedicate the launching ceremony in honor of Black History Month. Since individual efforts in the past had been fruitless, it was time to try for the last time. After all, my college life was nearing an end and I thought the last effort for me was to try and bridge the gap between Africans and black Americans. If ISO had succeeded in bridging the gap between foreign students and Americans, why couldn't OAS do the same for African and black Americans?

So we tirelessly worked day and night trying to prepare for the big day hoping it would score. The production team led by Charles Obwocha designed beautiful posters with full Africa color: red, green, black and gold. In honor of Black History Month, the posters read, *The Organization of African presents Festival of Arts and Culture.*

When I accompanied my treasurer to the Student Finance Board to request money for the event, they were so impressed by the posters that they approved the request almost automatically. In appreciation, I invited them to come and witness the real Africa as told by people who live it. No media slant, an Africa whose people are joyful for a minute without pictures of hunger, starvation and war.

We offered to feature traditional dances, an array of arts and crafts, food, plays and poetry. To encourage participation from our black American counterparts, we also extended an invitation to the Black Dance Company to perform.

Despite a few hurdles, everything went off well considering it was our first festival. Terry Rodenberg, the organization sponsor, gave the opening remarks, welcoming faculty and staff. Next, it was my turn to extend the olive branch:

"Ladies and Gentlemen: Welcome to our first Festival of Arts and Culture:

'The future of OAS depends on a number of things. Personally, I believe the growth of an organization will depend on our collective participation. OAS will strive to establish and maintain close contacts between the various student groups. It will strive to create close contact and act as a bridge to Africa. It will be our role as ambassadors of Africa, to bring to you the rich and vibrant culture from the continent.

Lastly, I wish to call upon all student leaders to put their weight solidly behind OAS so as to guarantee the growth and continued existence of the organization, not only in name but also in effectiveness. We have a responsibility not only to ourselves but also to the societies from where we spring. No one will ever do this task for us, until we on our own accord accept the challenge.

I am sure I am not alone with this dream of unity. I am glad and optimistic that you will join me in this quest to uncover the riches and beauty of Africa beneath layers of unknown. Prepare yourselves now; get ready so that as one, in one voice, one destiny, we can say, "Africa rise, thy light has come."

The first meeting was a success. The organization had put Africa on the college map. People were interested in joining in order to learn more about Africa. But my hope of encouraging more black participation fizzled. The attendance of black students was insignificant. How could they dare do this? It was a tribute to black America. We spent hours on this, and they didn't show up. I gave up hope. But at least, we had succeeded in dedicating a premier production to Black History Month. I had hoped that someday, interest in Africa could start from one, and then spread like wildfire. But the creation of an African organization on campus increased the cultural diversity. It vindicated my premise that the culture and behavior of black people has largely been shaped by the environment.

Some may argue that all black people are the same. Yes, we are the same—we share a race and many of the same insecurities. Sometimes, I can be thought of as violent or a thief in the same way any other person of color may be. But all these generalizations are due much to ignorance and unfounded fears.

As much as I tried to bridge the gap between Africans and blacks, all was in vain. But I hope that someday, more of the students who come after us will learn more from each other instead of looking at each other as threats . . . that more black students will journey to Africa and see what it is really like . . . that more black Americans will see Africa devoid of the media creation . . . and that black Americans will strengthen their bonds to Africa.

When that day comes, what a joy it will be for Africa and black America. I can't wait.

11

THE CRUMBLING WALLS, WHERE DO I GO FROM HERE?

The transition from college to the real world did not come easy. One disadvantage with some of the students from African countries was that, with no student loans available one had to work in the summer to try to raise fees for the next semester in a field outside their area of study. For example, I spent all the summers working at the Physical plant, painting dormitories when students were away. On the other hand, the American students in my class spent every summer doing internships at no pay with prospective employers, something that eased their transition from college to industry. Second, American students had the advantage of establishing a large network of alumni who proved vital in time of job search.

One evening after spending the day searching for work, I sat with my eyes darting this way and that way. I rose and increased the volume of my stereo. The song kept playing. I pressed the repeat key on my CD player to let the music continue. In the meantime, I refilled my wineglass. It had been a long day. I needed something to numb my tense feelings and escape momentarily from reality. I feared opening my mail, as I expected nothing good. After applying for several jobs, nothing looked promising so far. The past week had been particularly discouraging.

But I opened the letter, thinking it might be what I just needed to cheer me up. It was from Marion Laboratories in Kansas City where I had sent my resume. I struggled to open it. My heart was pumping, almost skipping beats. Maybe I got the job; maybe not. I kept talking to myself. Finally, I gained enough courage to open the letter fully. I went though it very fast and then flushed it down the toilet. I listened and watched as the contents were chewed up. I did not need any more of this.

For the past four years, I had learnt how to handle success.

The glory days of being at the pinnacle of success. The glory days of being a student leader of a powerful and diverse organization. I was at the center of success. I was the person to see when new students came and wanted to know where the action was. Success in making friends, so many that sometimes I did not have time for all of them. But with this success, came pressure to perform. Pressure to be the role model. I had always to strive for perfection, sometimes at a cost. My life was an open page. Now, at the end of the road, I faced new challenges, losing friends I had made in college, putting up with turndowns in the job market. At some stage I began to wonder, whether after every personal interview, my race played any key. It could be argued that I was letting in thoughts of being a captive of my race. Sometimes faced with a pile of regrets, it was impossible to ignore such thoughts.

Frustrated, I sat for a minute sandwiched between hope and despair. I felt a grip of complete unsettledness. Soon they will come for me. I felt outside of country, race and space. I dove into my journal, scribbling what seemed to me a reasonable paragraph, so eerie but vivid and reflective.

When the bush, shrubs, Savannah grass is burning and smoke billows and shrieks into the Heavens blanketing the skies, where does the eagle land? Where does the eagle land?

One part of me said, "the show must go on," the other said, "give up." Sworn not to allow American racial politics to determine my destiny, by the same token I had sworn not to allow Kenyan politics to do it either. I pledged to crash either of these evils to pulp. I was through with school. I had tried to walk a thin line between races. At home, fire was burning. My country was at the crossroads. Leaders were fanning tribalism. I sat in my little room. I knew I had a degree in Chemistry and a sober mind. Home was not ready to take me back. Here in America, I was jobless and had only a duration of a year to land one or go back to graduate school.

At that very moment, I heard a knock on my door. My deep thought process was snapped all of sudden. I was not expecting anyone but rose to open the door anyway.

"Wazzup, brother?"

"Nothing much."

"Allah Akbar . . . Allah Akbar (God is great)."

"I've always seen you around but have not had time to talk with you. Do you have a minute?" asked my unexpected visitor.

"Yes."

"Can I come in then?" he asked as if he needed more time to explain himself.

My house had always been invaded by vendors, Jehovah's Witnesses, members of the Church of Jesus Christ Latter Day Saints, and so on. This time who could it be?

"Sure, come right in," I answered.

"My name is Kareem, Allah Akbar."

"You live next door, don't you?"

"Yeah, on weekends I go to the city."

"Kareem, that's a Moslem name isn't it?"

"Yes, what about you?"

"I am not a Moslem."

"I mean, your name."

"Ababio."

"Aba-bio? . . . that's cool. That is a cool African name. Brother, we must stick together."

I nodded in agreement. After a pause, he continued, "We must stick to our own."

"We must stick to our own," that sentence immediately brought a full realization of who my guest was and why I happened to be "the lost brother he wanted to save."

I soon was able to trace it down to a certain Sunday afternoon a few months earlier.

During my college days, I was sometimes invited to give speeches in area high schools. On one occasion, I was invited by members of the Amnesty International Club to give a speech on apartheid in South Africa. This came after the students had witnessed one of our cultural performances at Central Missouri State.

High school was always a tough place to give speeches. I preferred lower high or grade school students because they tended to be very attentive and curious. In high school, the attention span was from 30 minutes to one hour. After that, general restlessness usually developed. However, to selected audiences like this one, the experience was gratifying.

In this particular case, the president of the organization had brought her group to the Peace-One-World International Cultural Night in school. After watching and hearing me speak, she waited and asked me to autograph her copy of the program. Then she organized for my then vice president, Saleh, and me to visit her school.

My experience with the members of the Amnesty International was both emotional and eye-opening. I realized that the media had not informed most of them about what was really happening in South Africa. Coming from Africa, and having been in contact with a lot of South African exiles, I had a lot of knowledge and my information was almost firsthand. After a question and answer session, the president thanked us and extended an invitation for us to speak again.

Later that week, the president called to ask whether she could pay me a visit so we could discuss the situation in South Africa and what their organization could do to help. She offered to deliver the check for our appearance too. We agreed to meet at Dairy Queen. So that Sunday afternoon, we met at Dairy Queen and after getting some ice cream, we proceeded toward my place east of town. I led the way. As we neared my residence, I could see my neighbor peeping from his window as if in disgust. Having experienced several of these incidents in the past, I did not let this concern me. After he came out from his trailer, took a stroll and I could hear him say to his friend, "My man here is lost. He's got jungle fever." I pretended not to hear him. I am not sure whether my guest heard.

That afternoon, we talked on several issues ranging from apartheid in South Africa to racism in America. We touched on attitudes of black people toward Africans and Africa at large. I could not help admiring the young woman's forthrightness and openness to very sensitive issues such as racism. She told me she was open-minded but that her parents were from the old school. We ended the conversation with hopes of communicating once she was in college in Kirksville, Missouri. She then handed me $35.00 for our appearance at her school. Soon, it was almost 6 o'clock she was ready to go. As I opened the door to see her off, I could see my neighbor perched on the doorstep leading of his trailer. Pretended not to be looking, he nevertheless kept staring.

"See you later."

"Bye," I said as I walked back into my room.

So, on this evening several months later when my neighbor knocked on my door, I knew exactly what was in store for me. "Well, black people must stick together. Have you ever seen a copy of this Newsletter?" he asked, displaying a copy of *The Final Call*, a paper distributed by the nation of Islam. "I tell you, when you read this paper, you will change your mind. So you're in college or something?"

"No, I am done with college. What about you?"

"I want to be a minister of Islam."

Hmm . . . I knew exactly what this man was after. "Are you going home?" he finally asked.

"I want to but I am not sure."

"You want to stay here man, I always thought Africa was good."

"It was when I left."

"So you like it here in America?"

"Well, at least you have the freedom to say what you want."

"No shit like that over there?"

"No, we just have our share of dictators who only leave office through a bullet or death."

"Just like that dude Idi Amin . . . that was some dude. He was cool though."

"Cool? . . . How?" I queried knowing that my friend was speaking out of anger against white people. He felt that by taking revenge on white people Idi Amin was a hero. This was a black Muslim whose hero was Louis Farrakhan.

"He was something. I was watching this movie, 'The rise and fall of Idi Amin.' He kicked those British folks out, made them carry his ass. Then he kicked those Orientals out too."

"You mean Asians."

"Yeah. Those suckers are bad. You watched the movie 'Mississippi Masala?'"

"Yes."

"Then you should know what I mean, bro. These people come to this country and take our jobs. After that, they despise us. Have you ever dated one of their women?"

"Asian, you mean?"

"Yeah, them Orientals."

"No, but I have good friends who are Asian. I feel their culture has much to do with it. Even if they feel like dating out of their culture, they find themselves slaves of the same."

"What about you, have you tried to date a white girl?"

"Can't do that man. Black to black."

"You're a black racist, aren't you?"

"No I am not. You'll never understand what they've done to us throughout the years, you'll never understand. You know, man, I know a lot of sisters in case you want me to hook ya up. Remember, we got to stick together as black people," he repeated on his way out in reference to my association with a lot of white friends and controlled by black people. Where a black person dated a black girl. Where there was absolutely no contact with the white world. If I wanted that, why did I leave Africa to come to America? Did my neighbor know that a bad black man is as vicious as his white counterpart? Did he know that I was born and grew up in Kenya where I saw a black independent country turn into a tribal state? I started reviewing his words one by one and asked myself, "If Africa was good, then why I am staying here? Has the first home for man become the last place for man?"

Things in my country were at a crossroads. One of Africa's longest-ruling dictators, Arap Moi of Kenya, had reluctantly unbanned the opposition in response to mounting pressure from western donors and government critics. On the face of it it looked like democracy was finally coming to roost. However, the secret police was experienced in clamping down the opposition. They gave true meaning to the rule of fear and silence.

My hopes of returning home to build a young independent country were dwindling by the minute. First my family had relations with the opposition, so Arap Moi would be sure to thwart any efforts they made to succeed. It was not by coincidence that at some forums, while still in school, I had spoken publicly against Moi's regime. One of these came after the brutal murder of Kenya's foreign minister, who was my inspiration and role model. The sudden disappearance and death of one of my heroes added fuel to injury. At this time I thought of publishing a poem I had written called "The House of the Republic." The poem could have landed me in jail in Kenya at that time as it might be deemed as bordering on sedition, something punishable by detention without trial. I always wanted to be a journalist but feared being one in Kenya where most writers were locked up for writing anything critical of the government. So despite all the encouragement from my high school English and literature teachers, I went against their wishes. After deciding to pursue a degree in chemistry, my hope was to later on polish up my writing career as a hobby.

Looking back, I recalled my tenure as editor of the Mwananchi, how I came to realize that though we shared a lot as Kenyan students, the Moi government had found a way to send student spies to infiltrate the organization. In a special edition to commemorate madaraka (self-government) day, we decided to devote it mostly to the role of students in national development. We also printed the articles in the U.S. press on Kenya.

Articles came from students opposed to Moi's regime. I collected articles from the *Christian Science Monitor*, *The New York Times*, and *Africa Confidential*, a publication based in London but banned in Kenya. Headlines included, "Moi Clamps Opposition, "Secret weapon deployed,"

"Kenya gears for ballot." The features editor, who happened to be from Moi's tribe, was reluctant to contribute articles for the newsletter, determined to keep his name out of the fray.

With government spies operating everywhere, I knew that my future in Kenya was out. However, I was fearless. I was prepared to face the consequences. I spent sleepless nights compiling articles to be read not only by Kenyans but also by all friends of the Kenya student community. The situation had reached a point where hiding the truth and lying about our country was meaningless. How long could we stand on the sidelines and watch the game as spectators instead of playing the game?

The newsletter caused uproar. I encountered Kenya's own right wing in form of pro-government students who had bought up to the fact that multiparty in Kenya would lead to ethnic chaos. "What is this?" one retorted angrily. "How dare you print this? This is a shame. I will mail a copy to the embassy."

"What's wrong with it?"

"Is this what you're telling Americans?"

"But how long can we hide it, don't they read the papers? Mind you, that is a straight copy from the 'Monitor.'"

"Bwana, this is shit." The spokesman for the group picked up several copies and mumbled something in his dialect. He had increasingly become hot as if his mouth hid a bowl of pepper. He had taken it too personally and had no time to reason. I was in no and asked that I retract the contents of the editorial. I agreed to attend but in defense of the newsletter. At no point was I going to apologize for telling the truth.

I walked into that room in the company of Ndunge, a Kenyan lady friend. We were two versus 15 other members of the Kenyan Students Association. The KSA president, Mr. Kidwaro brought the meeting to order. The room was silent, everyone appearing ready to strike. The president remained neutral though I knew he was on my side. I was the target. I was like a wounded tiger ready to defend my individualism.

"Do you stand by what you wrote?" one of them asked.

"I do stand by it not only in part, but also in every sense of the word, it is the truth," came my reply.

"How can you write this rubbish . . . eh? . . . What will they say in Kenya?"

"Truth, do you believe this American propaganda?"

"Most of it is correct. It is time we looked at what the rest of the world says about us."

"Why not write about tourism?"

"Tourism will not exist without political stability, the two go hand in hand," somebody mumbled in his dialect.

"No more newsletters if this is what we get."

"That's fine with me, but you know the truth hurts. We can no longer hide the truth.

"We must leave politics alone. We are all grown-ups and must agree to argue without losing our cool". The president concluded the meeting by adjourning the heated and terse exchange. I walked away feeling like a stranger within my own people. I had spent many years in a foreign land thinking that I had overcome tribalism, but this night I felt like a lone traveler. I realized that the evils of tribalism had been inflicted on the generation supposed to move the country onto the world stage. I walked away dejected, thinking, "If I feel like a stranger within my own people, how can I feel before the world?"

I had walked from the cocoons and walls of tribe; I had walked from the borders of my country into the open lands only to discover that the tribal feuds from my native land had raised their ugly heads again. As in the case of racism, the serpent of tribalism had only been scorched, not burnt. "Is this what we have become? Is this what I would be coming home to face? It is worth it? I've tried to run away from this. If this is the shape of the future, then I'd rather not be part of it," I declared.

Sitting in my room reflecting on the past, I looked at my failures and past successes. My glory days, from being a nonentity to becoming a powerful voice in the university. I rose to refill my wine glass. The music from the CD kept playing. I looked at the clock on the wall. It registered half past seven. Since it was my off day, I took it easy and raised the volume. Tonight I am going to dance, I am going to dance and escape from reality. I am not going to think about the letter, I told myself. Tomorrow, I'll drive to the big city. Tomorrow I will leave for the big city. I'm armed with hope and strong recommendations.

Tomorrow I'll walk into corporate America. I will try to penetrate and be part of the system for I have no other place to go. Tomorrow I'll be on the road in search of the way forward. I'll be on the road in search of the answer to the question, "Where do I go from here?"

12

INTO CORPORATE AMERICA THE GREAT WIDE OPEN

I moved to Kansas City with a few hours of research left before graduating. That meant I had to commute to school once a week to run an experiment with my professor, the head of the chemistry department. I was under extreme pressure to do well since he had the final say. My efforts were rewarded as after my oral presentation, I received a letter from him saying that my research work was acceptable. He continued to urge me to consider graduate school and use him as a reference. He too encouraged me to use the high percentile score I had obtained on the external exit exam. How deeply I wanted to get that Ph.D.; however, I had bills to pay. So I decided to put grad school off for a year in favor of taking a job in industry.

I got a job with an adhesive company soon after graduation and arrival in Kansas City. The hiring process was so quick that I got scared. I had the title of a research chemist, carried a business card and was salaried. The pay was good, so I thought here was my start. After all the regrets, here was my chance. I could pay off my car, leftover student loans and even credit cards.

All was well for four months until the person whom I had relieved was back from maternity leave. When she returned, we were fighting for the same job. Sometimes we had nothing to do, so we ended up testing samples over and over. I started feeling that my stint with the company was going to be a short one.

Sure enough. One day I was called to the controller's office. "Ababio, have a seat."

"Thank you."

"Well, I am going to fire you."

"What . . . why. I thought you recently applauded me for doing a superb job?"

"I am under instruction from the top. I am going to pay you for the next two weeks and give you this letter of recommendation."

"But . . . I've some bills to clear. Can't you give me at least a month?"

"No, I cannot afford to pay two people for one person's job."

"Well, thank you."

"Ababio, I have nothing to do with this. I work here too."

"I understand," I said as I took the letter and left like a wounded dog with his tail between his legs. I walked past the secretary toward the locker room where under watchful eyes of a senior chemist I emptied and bagged my belongings. I surrendered the lab coats and entry badge, then I proceeded toward the exit. From the corner of my eye, I could see the secretary giving me a helpless look. She always said hello to me in the morning and after work. She was obviously wishing she could help.

As I sat in my car and looked at the building for the last time, I cut open the letter of recommendation to see the contents. My fears were laid to rest after reading it and realizing that I was not in the wrong but, like a lot of Americans, a victim of a lay-off. I was advised to proceed to the Division of Employment Security to receive unemployment benefits. But that was not going to be enough to pay the bills. Here I was on the road again. After getting used to my own apartment, I had to move in with a friend and share the costs. My business cards found their way into the gutter. I had to start over again.

Life was harder without a job. The hardest part was the transition. Waking up without going to work was something I found hard to handle. Nevertheless, after I woke up in the morning, I dressed well like a jobseeker and then proceeded to the unemployment office to check on openings. If there were none, I'd go to the library to read. I mostly read articles on how to handle job loss, how to stay focused and keep stress at bay. I wanted to stay in high spirits with the hope that an opportunity would knock on my door someday. In the meantime, I mailed resumes and made phone calls. I used the resources at the library and at the employment office. As my job search continued, I thought of going to grad school. I applied and was admitted to pursue a degree in pharmaceutical chemistry. In the meantime, I was going broke.

The decision to go to graduate school or industry was a tough one. My situation was such that I needed money quickly not only to clear my bills but to help my family. I was receiving calls from bill collectors who were all after me. To add insult to injury, I was soon falling out of legal immigration status if I did not get a job soon to change my visa. My other option was to take classes.

Things kept getting worse by the day as one day I woke up in the morning and found my car gone. I panicked thinking it had been stolen. I took the phone and filled a report with the police. They told me that the car was not stolen but had been repossessed. They gave me the address of the lot where to get it back but with the condition that I had $2000.00. That was that amount left on the loan. Otherwise, the other option was to go and collect my possessions. I did not have that amount of cash on me. So I asked my roommate, Bobga for a ride to go and reclaim my possessions.

Finally, I landed an interview with a company. This was followed by a second and third interview. I got the job, thanks to strong recommendations from my references, including my previous employer. I accepted the offer at half the salary of my previous job and put grad school on hold since I could not do my program part-time.

My next obstacle after the job was getting means of transportation. With a repo record on my credit, it was hard to get a new car immediately. I arranged to borrow a car from a Kenyan friend in Columbia, Missouri who had an extra old car. On my off-day the following weekend, I got a ride from my roommate to pick up the car.

After a couple of months, I was on my feet again. I paid off essential outstanding bills and got myself a used car. At work, things started looking bright as a higher paying position opened up after one of the employees left to go to medical school. My supervisor asked me whether I was willing to take the job. "It is all yours if you're interested," She added. The decision was simple, and my answer was an automatic yes.

Despite years in America, I still had the hangover of extended family. I had to tr y pushing my younger brothers to avoid dependency in the future. So my plans to get that Ph.D. were permanently put on hold. I opted to work my way up in industry and once eligible, try getting a higher degree to enable me to move up within the company.

I worked hard, and even took an extra part-time job as a pizza delivery driver in the evenings to enable me to save enough money to visit home after almost nine years.

13

I AM GOING HOME

Finally, the day for me to go home had come. During my ten- year stay in America, I never ceased to receive requests to visit.

Yet whenever I had the desire to do so, money was always not enough. I tried working two jobs; still the money went to bills. It was always one thing after the other. There was a time when I wanted to visit so badly. Things were getting bad at home, and I had kept silent for long because I was so helpless financially to support myself, leave alone the myriads of financial demands from home. Like an infant, helpless to act, I went underground for almost a year. My family was so worried they thought something bad had happened to me. Finally, I got courage and made a phone call to ask them for more patience. They obliged. And so I saved some money for a return ticket. I sacrificed everything. Within a year of sacrifice and driving a used ragged car, I saved enough money not only for a ticket but also for some desktop publishing equipment. And so on December 11, 94, I was ready to go.

I got a ride to the airport. I had so much luggage I almost needed a truck. I had three computers with monitors, a plotter and several printers on top of the usual gifts for my family, bringing the total to 12 pieces. I had started a computer business while searching for stable employment, and needed the equipment to establish a desktop publishing bureau at home. This way, I could operate it from my base in the U.S. but still enable my family to work over there. Although it was not my major in school, I had become introduced to technology through friends who had learned it on their own.

I arrived at the airport an hour before departure time. With this much luggage and boarding an international flight, I needed that much time for clearance.

"Your passport and ticket please," the attendant at the American Airlines terminal stated, eyeing my luggage in disbelief.

"Here, sir," I handed over my traveling documents as politely as possible.

"Is all this your luggage?"

"Yes, sir."

"Are you aware that you are only allowed two pieces and a carry-on?"

"Yes, sir I will pay the rest as excess baggage."

"It will cost you," he concluded, paused and proceeded to the next customer.

I went to the weighing ramp where I presented my travel documents again, this time to the ticket counter officer. The short, stout man regarded my documents and started weighing them one by one.

"It is over by only 3 pounds, what do you want to do?"

"I will remove some items," I said.

"OK, move out of the line, then come back after you're done. We've got to keep the line moving. Next."

I moved to the side and removed some things from one suitcase and transferred them to the other. I was guessing about the weight since I did not have a scale. Time was running out. It was now approximately 30 minutes to our departure time. I returned to the line and got stuck in the rear. I was getting impatient but tried to be as calm as possible. I am usually very patient, so this was still below my threshold.

"Ready this time?"

"Yes," I replied, trying to hide my displeasure. The attendant weighed my luggage again, one by one. One of the suitcases had now gone up one pound over the limit.

"It is over by one," he fought to say. He seemed tired of doing the whole thing again, so to avoid delaying the other customers, he tallied the total excess baggage and asked me to pay $600 dollars. I had expected to pay about that much so it was no problem.

On receiving the money, he labeled the packages and gestured me to proceed toward the departure lounge. I waved off my ride and went on.

After the formal security clearance I was finally en route to Kenya via Chicago and Frankfurt, Germany. In Chicago, I disembarked the AA flight and hurried toward the baggage claim area. Since I had 12 pieces, I had to enlist the use of an airport cab attendant.

"You need help carrying all these?"

"Yeah, just a minute." I took time to look at him and assure myself he was genuine. Knowing how susceptible a traveler can be to an unsuspecting conman, I checked his badge and noticed he had contracted with AA. In case anything went wrong, I now had his name and badge number.

"I need these ferried to the Lufthansa terminal," I finally stated.

"Lufthansa, cool. I know where that is. You from Africa, man?"

"Yeah."

"That's cool. I thought for sure you was not from here. You're from the motherland. Eh?" he continued.

"Yeah."

"I have always wanted to go there for a visit, but I can't afford it. But one of these days I am going to make it."

"That should be nice."

"Yeah, I've heard it is pretty nice there, man. My friend went to Ghana and was impressed. I can't wait to go myself."

"Would be nice."

Soon we were at the Lufthansa terminal. He dropped off the first six pieces of my baggage and went to get the rest. Having been assured by AA that he was one of their contracted employees, I had no more worries. In the meantime, I sat watching over my luggage. The attendant at the Lufthansa check-in counter was a no-nonsense Germany lady. To her everything was serious business. Soon my last six pieces arrived and I was ready to check in.

"Next," she called as I was finalizing matters with my AA contractor.

"How much is it?" I asked.

"Just give me what you feel is good enough."

Without any hesitation, I gave him 50 dollars. He had no questions. He thanked me profusely and gave me his contact information. "If you happen to be in Chicago, this is my phone number, ok!"

"Thank you, man," I said in appreciation not only for his help but for wanting to keep in contact. It assured me that the guy was for real. During my stay in the United States, I had not often encountered black people with a desire to visit Africa. By getting this kind of treatment from my own, I was touched. First, he did not put money ahead of everything. Second, he was willing to visit Africa.

I turned my head from the man pushing the cart, to the lady at the ticket counter.

"Sorry, I was just finishing up with him," I said apologetically.

"The flight leaves in 30 minutes."

"I am sorry, madam." I sensed some fear, the fear that occurs when the color of your skin becomes defamation and betrayal.

"These packages are not sealed properly," she complained as she took some heavy-duty tape and resealed the boxes. She then tallied the amount of excess baggage and asked me to pay $1,200. I had six hundred in cash on me and my card was almost at the limit. I sure did not have 600 dollars on that card.

"What do we do?" She asked impatiently.

"I'm sorry, but I don't have that much money on me," I exclaimed.

"Call the credit card company." She directed me to the nearest public phone. I hurried pulled an ATT calling card and called the card company. I was put on hold for a while. I hung up and made a different call to a friend to try find an alternative solution. I called to ask him to pick up the excess luggage and store it for me till I return. But reaching a decision on what to leave was the hardest part. My friend was not at home so I left a message on his answering machine. I now noticed the lady at the counter waving me to hurry. It looked as if she was trying to say something rather impatiently. All the passengers were lining up. Desperately, I called the card company again. Now a line was forming outside the booth. This time I got through on the first try. I met a friendly voice at the other end and requested an overdraft as my card was over the limit. She asked me how much over the limit. "Six hundred," I said.

"Wait while I consult with my credit manage," was her reply.

After a short, nervous wait, she came back and told me to have the people at the counter call her in case of any problems. My hopes were up. My heart was racing. I dashed toward the ticket counter. I could hear over the intercom a voice announcing the departure of flight LF11 for Frankfurt. It was now 15 minutes to departure time.

"You've got it approved?"

"Yes, and they asked you to call this number to get the approval. The attendant lifted her phone in disgust and paged someone to load the cargo into the plane. It looked as if she was ready to approve the shipment whatever happened. She took the card, scanned it and waited for the transaction to complete. To the amazement of us all, it went through right away.

"Run to the boarding lounge, you've only got five minutes."

"What about all my luggage?"

"Worry about that in Nairobi."

With that assurance, I dashed though the long escalator leading into a rotunda-shaped departure lounge on my way to Frankfurt. After several hours in the air, the fasten seatbelt light suddenly came on. The turbulence grew intense. The flight attendants kept assuring us that everything was fine. In the center aisle next to me a restless child kept crying as his mother handed him a toy as a bargain for silence. The little boy became every more agitated by the turbulence, which had the whole plane shaking. Even a stranger to church at this point needed a little time to consult with God. I remembered the Psalms of David:

> I will lift mine eyes into those hills and my help cometh from
> God Maker of heaven and Earth

Soon the lights were turned off again, and from my window seat. I could see some rays of morning light filtering through the thick clouds. In front of me the flight screen indicated we were over Yugoslavia and the Swiss Alps. Sarajevo, my heart almost missed a beat. What if some stinger missile headed our way? What if?

The next thing I heard were the words Auf Wiedersehn from the flight crew. I looked at my watch and saw it was early morning. I was halfway home. I proceeded to the arrival terminal to catch my connecting flight to Nairobi.

At 18:00 hrs, Lufthansa flight LK11 landed at Embakasi Airport in Nairobi. As it taxied toward the arrival terminal, a voice with a strong

German accent said, "Ladies and gentlemen, this is our final destination. I hope you enjoyed your flight. We wish you a happy stay and thanks for flying Lufthansa. Auf Wiedersehn."

The tropical sun was plunging out of the earth. The moon made its way over the trees from the horizon. The gentle wind blew in the trees surrounding the flight terminal. From one end of the airport, a fire truck came rolling on a routine patrol.

On my way toward the arrival lounge, I saw the familiar welcome signs, *Karibuni*. At the same time, the airport police clutched their guns at the ready as if the passengers posed a security threat. Nevertheless, I was so excited I walked past them without filing my clearance papers.

"Wapi fomu yako?" the customs officer asked impatiently as I handed him my passport.

"Fomu gani? (Which form?)"

"You need to fill out that form there," he said directing me to the forms on a desk in the middle of the room. I filled out the forms and joined the queue again. I towed behind 10 other arrivals. But soon it was my turn. I took my passport together with the entry form and handed them to the customs officer. The man regarded them as if trying to detect the slightest reason to turn me down. Finding none, he stamped my passport and waved me to proceed toward the baggage claim area.

There were huge crowds along the claim area. My eyes darted hither and thither trying to spot a familiar face. Finally as I walked past the partition toward the adjoining area, a voice shrieked from the crowd "Ndio yule." (He's there).

I walked past the lady in front of me trying to identify the voice more clearly. At the same time the crowd surged forward. The security police tried to turn them back. I broke my way into the crowd and got swallowed in a melee. I hugged my family one by one. My nephews ran and took care of my luggage. For a moment, my thoughts went back several years.

"You will come back," . . . a voice from the crowd then had asked.

"Yes," I replied pushing back tears, "in 10 years I will be back."

"Remember us."

"I will . . . I will never forget you."

"Will you write?"

"I will . . . I promise . . . I will."

As if prophetic, after 10 years I was back.

I got hold of my three-year-old niece, Oprah, who had handed me a bouquet of flowers. "So this is what home feels like," I commented to myself. Tomorrow I will be at Kenyatta market feasting on nyama choma (grilled beef), tomorrow I'll be dancing and enjoying a sweet family togetherness. "Tomorrow," the word seemed stuck in my mind. Suddenly I turned my head to the twinkling city lights as the driver sped past the security roadblocks, then to the dark and winding road ahead of me, and to the future.

I turned to my other niece, Sheila, whom time had transformed from an infant to a beautiful teenager.

"How is America, uncle?" she asked shyly trying to discover the uncle she has been told about. "Ni kama hapa tu,"(America is like here), I said trying to wrestle with my native language. She laughed and said, "Kumbe hujasahau Kiswahili" (Sure, you haven't forgotten the language).

14

HOME, WHERE ARE YOU? (NYUMBANI, YU WAPI)

Days went by very fast. Each day I met friends from the past but we did not have a lot to share but questions about America.

They asked whether there was an abundance of money in America. They asked about job opportunities in America and wanted to know possibilities of coming to America. Most expressed frustration about life in Kenya. They talked of lack of opportunities, scarcity of basic items. The more they asked all these questions, the more they made me feel that I was better staying in America. I answered their questions, avoiding the hard realities of African immigrants in America. I did this to give them hope. I was jealousy of America to even mention my hard struggles and incidents of racism and apathy from African Americans. I told them the good parts, the good experiences, the freedom to express one's own political expression without fear of police harassment. The ability to live in a house without a fenced barricade.

As we socialized with friends, I realized that those who were asking me to return had it made in one way or the other. Their connection to people in higher echelons of government made it possible for them to afford luxuries out of reach to regular people.

Every day I read the newspapers, I read of strikes and layoffs. And yet some people had it really good. They owned satellite dishes; they could afford membership in social clubs unthinkable to an average person. They drove imported cars.

One evening, a friend from high school heard I was in town and asked me to meet with him at an exclusive club in Nairobi. We agreed to meet there on Sunday after church. It is a few minutes from the heart of the city. I had to go to church at home, which was a serious ritual during my boyhood days. It still is as I came to find out. Though I always found an excuse to avoid it during my boyhood days, I had to do this to convince my parents that I still obeyed their wishes by going to church. Even out of their sight and control, I still went to church in America depending on my work schedule. One reason why I avoided going to church during my boyhood days was that it took too long. We went in at 9:00am and came out at 2:00pm. The preacher ignored the basic stomach demands for a lunch meal. This made us look for excuses of skipping church. Sometimes I would say, "laundry was not done" or say "I had a headache." To make the latter a valid excuse made sure the headache started on Saturday night, just before going to bed. Amazingly, by 3:00pm on Sunday it was out.

That Sunday afternoon we went to City Cabanas for lunch. My brother drove me there since it was hard for me to drive on the right hand side of the street as in most former British colonies. It was a fifteen minute drive.

When we arrived we meet groups of well-to-do Kenyans spending a relaxed afternoon with their families. In addition, there were flocks of European and American tourists. We took a table at the corner and signaled the waiter to come to our table.

It took a bit long and we were growing impatient as most waiters paid more attention to the tables flocked by European and American tourists as they thought they could get hefty tips. Did he know I was from America too?

I wondered. Here I was, strange as it may seem, in my own country and could not even get good service. I had thought after so many years away, things had changed.

We were free but yet mentally enslaved. I swore not to tip the waiter. I could that way validate his initial suspicion.

"Sasa bwana Ababio, America vipi? (What is up men, how is America)" Mulei burst in.

"Sawa tu (fine), I replied.

"Si unaona, hata sisi tumeendelea (As you can see, we have progressed too)."

"Kweli, (true)."

He gestured the reluctant waiter to our table.

He ordered Nyama choma, and to drink Tusker. I opted for a Woodpecker, wine cooler.

"Now when are you coming back?"

"I am back."

"I mean for good."

"I will always come again."

"Bwana, things are good here, ask Shem."

"Things for sure looked good for a few." He drove an expensive Mercedes Benz. He lived in a reclusive neighborhood in the city. He owned a satellite dish and seemed to watch all the TV programs we have in the States. Yet people like my brother were looking for a way out. Not that they did not have all the right qualifications, but because some higher up from such and such tribe wanted to promote his own.

As the afternoon progressed and the bottle was taking effect, Mulei started boasting about his possessions. He asked me to look at his suit, which he had imported from London and asked me whether I knew where he can get supplies of the same brand in the United States. "Yes, but at a cost," I said. "Money is not a problem," he replied. He told me how he got all imported things from Dubai, in the United Arab Emirates. I did not have much to say since I knew that an average man in Kenya with a normal wage could hardly make ends meet.

Mulei extended an invitation to me to go see some of the properties he had here and there.

"I am going up country tomorrow, maybe after that, if my schedule allows," I replied.

"Thanks for everything," I said as we rose to leave.

"All the time, Karibu Nyumbani" (Welcome home) he replied, reaching for his wallet to clear the bill.

As we drove through the city that evening and the sun had sent forth its last ray, I looked at Uhuru and Haile Selassie avenues, the bougainvilleas along the avenues during my boyhood days at the Polytechnic were now all gone. Everything looked out of place. Tall buildings had mushroomed all over the city. "This one here, owned by so and so," my brother kept pointing out to me. All the owners were connected to the ruling Party.

In the meantime, melee crowds scrambled for matatus to the residential estates. The matatus ran amok without paying attention to stop signs. As we drove toward the estate, I was scared inside and my soul was being pulled away. When I was in America, I missed home. I always waited for a chance to touch and even kiss the native soil. Strangely, I missed America. In America, I had made a little group of friends, all adrift and without definite place to call home. Friends who shared the same feelings and some form of alienation. In America, I made friends, immigrants from other countries who felt their hopes of returning to settle in native countries dimmed and exile to them had become a form of life. In America I had found a group of friends, playmates, co-workers, African exiles, immigrants from different countries and Americans who became a kind of family. In this little community of foreigners we shared a past and maybe a future away from home. Before realizing, we were in the house. I retired to bed earlier to be ready for an up country trip the next day.

The next morning, we went up country. We drove through the beautiful countryside. We drove through Nakuru. The buildings the roads were in awful shape and my heart was jumping nervously as the car we maneuvered to avoid this pothole and that. Soon we were in the countryside home. I am glad we arrived at night to avoid curious onlookers who were ready to see the uncle who had come from America. As it is with most young Kenyans, up country is a place where people go at Christmas to see their parents and grandparents. People usually stay in the urban areas where there are employment opportunities. So whenever one goes up country, there's a general curiosity by the rural folk to see what someone from America had brought. I did not know how the word got out that I was arriving. At any rate, I was unsuccessful in steaming off the relatives who came in to meet me and make numerous requests. Some thought since I was in America where money was abundant, I was their Santa. Some wanted me to find their children admission in America. Apart from my uncle who insisted that I visit him at his home, the rest of the people came home and met with me.

Later that evening, we went to his place. My old uncle who sat there, surrounded by grandkids who listened attentively to see whether I had changed.

"Son, there in America do they have ugali and sukuma wiki like here?"

"Yes, they have everything like here," I answered trying so hard to prove I was still the same.

"Kweli?" (True).

"There, we have anything you can get, even snow."

"Snow, must be cold, do you go to work during the snow period?"

"Nothing stops, we go to work as usual."

"Wazungu, hao *ni watalaamu*." (Americans are geniuses). After a week, it was my time to bid farewell and leave up country for Nairobi, from where I had to depart the country for the second time. All this time I felt something was missing. I felt some disconnection while visiting home as most of the friends we had gone to high school with had all run out of the country and are scattered all over the world in search of opportunities. I felt at home and yet alone.

Finally, a month from the time I entered the country, my family escorted me to the airport. They had many requests and encouraged me to work hard and help get the rest of the family across. They did not ask me to come back. Instead, they envied my opportunity to be in America. I then bid everyone goodbye, but my little niece refused to let go.

"Take me with you," little Oprah broke in, finding her way to my lap.

"To America?"

"Yes, I want to go Uncle", she added.

"Na shule?" (And school).

"Nitaenda shule huko", (I'll go to school there).

"Sawa", (Fine), I said, to avoid squelching her excitement. They finally held her back with a promise that I will come for her on my next visit. I dashed toward the departure lounge into the awaiting Lufthansa plane.

As I sat in the plane, I reflected on the changes in the landscape from my boyhood days. I realized how staying away had really changed me. Though I could not notice it, change had taken place. I seriously thought of ways to bring my family with me because it was the only connection I had with my native land. If I had to carry them away with me and closely watch my parents grow old instead of being miles away. I wished and wished.

I felt despite love for country, I was being pulled by something strong, search for inner peace and security. I was being pulled away from barricades and insecurity.

Home, where are you? The question kept coming on my mind. Is it where I was born and spent my boyhood days or is it where I have seen the unfolding of my adult life, the unfolding of freedom and liberty? Gone is the beautiful land of my boyhood days. I was sandwiched between these warring forces, one patriotic one and the other to the place where I have become a man. A place where my manhood had awakened, and life was unfolding before my very eyes. With the naked realities of the moment, the choice was not hard to make.

Without realizing it, we were in Frankfurt, Germany. I got off the place and dashed toward my connection flight to the States. At the airport lounge, I encountered myriads of people trying to look for an American visa. Some had been sleeping there waiting for deportation. I felt I was lucky to have a green card and I had to go through the blue line for American citizens and permanent residents. I no longer would be scrambling to queue along the visitors and non-citizen line.

At 1:00 pm I disembarked from the plane and in front of me sprayed from the skies, the Statue of Liberty. I was in New York again. This time without fear.

FOREWARD PART II

In part two of his memoir, the author, on returning from home and settling in America has to grabble with day-to-day challenges where he sometimes has to ask himself in trying to make it whether he's a captive or a victim of race. He argues that the environment determines how far one can go. One can climb greater heights of accomplishment provided the conditions are right. *In Beyond a Race, Beyond a Tribe*, the author sets forth his desire to go through life like a swan gliding between tribe, culture and race without being a captive. He explores, tribal, culture and race relations in his native country and how tribalism and cultural apartheid are to Africa what racism is to America.

In *Chances Are*, he argues that despite the challenges facing an immigrant of African origin, sometimes feelings sandwiched be- tween two opposing forces, with hard work one has the potential to succeed. In the next chapter, *The Bonds That Bind Us*, he argues that African-Americans have the potential of doing to Africa what the Jews have done to Israel—they have the ability to strengthen the bonds with Africa. In *Where my Country Fell Short with Me*, he laments that his native country, like any other African countries, offers no opportunities for either the educated or the young, espe- cially not for anybody with opposing political points of view. As a result, many highly skilled individuals have been marooned to exile. In *And Yet I Keep on Walking*, he ends with a call for togeth- erness and hope that, however arduous the struggle, America of- fers a chance to pursue one's dream.

PART II

REFLECTIONS

15

CAPTIVE OR VICTIM OF MY RACE?

I s it me against the world or is the world against me? As a black one is left with one of the two. Some might argue that black people have same rights as white people and deserve no special privileges. It might too be argued that a black man has been a victim of slavery, colonization, and apartheid. Both of these arguments might be true. Coming from an African country, I have experienced both situations. There are times when I have been a victim of the stereotypes against black people. There have been times when I have felt uneasy going to some banks to borrow money because of fear that the application will be denied solely because I fit the profile. There have been times when I have been stopped on the road by a police officer because I fit the profile of a middle aged black man they have been looking for. There have been cases in searching for a residential apartment when I have been asked to put a deposit higher that what is usually asked for white prospects. In all these cases I have been a victim.

On the other side of the coin, there have been cases where a lot of people have paid the price to help the lazy crowd. There have been cases whereby the system that was created to help those people who rightly needed help has been misused and sometimes abused. Such has been the welfare system. I have come to realize that some racial tensions have been heightened by the fact that people go to work every day only to see a large part of their income go to aid the low income groups. Going back to slavery days, it so happens that a black man had been disadvantaged to the fact that he lags behind in economic terms that he becomes the recipient of the welfare benefits. And with this comes the wrath of the white society.

As an African and black man, I have to live with this. I wake up each day and go to work to prove that I don't fit the stereotype. I have to work even harder to prove that given the same tools, I can achieve the same result. But sometimes, not all can succeed in this quest. Some people might get frustrated and be so mad at society. Some divert their hatred and frustration to the white society. Such is the case of Oga, a former student at Central Missouri State University. I have referred to him simply as Oga in here to maintain his privacy. Oga came to this country after spending most of his life in Nigeria. He had worked in his home country until one day he got an opportunity to come and get a degree in America. At his age, it was hard to learn any new habits and adjust to the new surroundings. He was inflexible and was unable to shed parts of his culture to learn new ideas and adjust to American way of life. Whenever he asked for anything with a deep accent and was misunderstood, he became so infuriated and impatient. His life in college became a torment. He hated the American society.

After graduation, Oga moved to the city in search of work. He searched and searched but whenever he went for an interview, he was not called back. He felt betrayed by his deep accent that could not help him secure a job in corporate America. He finally got a job driving cab. One afternoon, I went to the airport and met Oga. After exchanging greetings, I asked him how he was doing.

"Things are badoo," he replied.

"Been home since Warrensburg days?"

"Man, I was in Nigeria and things are really badoo. I was at this hotel in Lagos one evening. Since I was from America I thought I would have a chance to talk to my Nigerian woman. But to my surprise, they flocked the tables of American tourists. I lost my temper and confronted the one white man and warned him not to talk to my sister. You did not want me in your country and you are here chasing my woman. Go back to America. To my amazement, the woman told me to shut up and mind my own business. She added that it was her choice to go out with the white man. I was mad and dejectedly walked away. I felt betrayed by what I had thought was my country and women. A month later, I was on my way back and here I am driving cab."

"That is the reality Oga. You run away from one jail only to enter another. Africa has changed a lot since we left. I don't know about you, but I think it takes two to tangle. I for a long time thought I would be in Kenya today in some form of managerial position, but the reality is, here I am. I've learnt to appreciate the little things in life. I have learnt to make the best that this society offers. There are opportunities here. Don't give up yet. Keep knocking on those doors, maybe something will come up."

"That why I came back." he said as he drove off to pick up a customer.

In Oga's case, we see him both as a victim and a captive of race. His lack of willingness to be flexible and adapt to American way of life makes it harder for Americans to reach up to him and see him on face value. He stubbornly sticks to his culture and yet he's in America, a country with a different culture. He is insecure about himself and feels that the fact that he cannot find a chance in corporate America is due to the fact that he's African and black. He's captivated by this fact that for anything that is not right blame must go to the white society. This might not be totally true. Oga has realized from his trip to Nigeria that betrayals and let downs are everywhere from his own country to his own people. He has run away from the society he calls home to the society he hated and thought was always against him. Oga is not alone but a reflection of so many Africans who find themselves in this strange paradox.

Looking back at my college days at Central, It was not easy trying to balance these two forces. In America, there were a lot of stereotypes about black people. Some of these started from an earlier age. When I left home, I had thought that in college I could have a chance to see the other side.

Coming from Kenya, a black country, I had thought coming to a majority white college, I'll have a chance to reach the other side. See what is on the other side of the road. I thought I would have a chance of learning what inter-cultural dating meant. So in college, I wanted to have a change to explore this. To do this therefore, dating a Kenyan girl could not give me a chance to learn about the white culture. Second, after leaving the country, on one knew how long my stay in this country was going to be. It was not an easy feat in a racially polarized campus.

The suspicions and fears between black and whites at Central led to different sitting arrangements in the cafeteria. Blacks sat in one corner, whites in the other. Foreigners, myself included, sat in the white area or could be found anywhere. Sometimes the Chinese were alone at their own table conversing in their own tongues. Similarly, Indians students sat on their own table carrying their conversation in Hindu or some language comprehensible to a select few.

In this room, college was transformed into distinct cultural homelands between which the distinctive border was language. For me, an African and black, the obvious expectation was that I would be in the black area or the African table. However, this was not the case. One day I might be sitting with some Chinese students from Nickerson Hall, the next day with some Africans, and at yet another time with some Americans, especially returning students who shared a dorm with me. Some of these students had been overseas and had developed an insatiable desire to learn about new cultures. I was not alone; other Africans found themselves in the same predicament.

One day I was sitting with some Chinese students when suddenly, from an adjacent table, I overheard bitter and sarcastic comments.

"Is that dude a geek?" a black student asked his friends.

"Might be one of them Shaka Zulu's from Ethiopia," the other replied as in a mock reproach.

Sitting with the Chinese, I did not understand a single word of their conversation; however, that was a sacrifice I had to pay in order to get along. I had to develop the ability to glide like a swan between black and white worlds, touching down everywhere in between, neither as a stranger nor as a captive of my race. I wanted to learn all cultures but not at an expense of my own. I wanted to share my past experiences with people who were ready to open up share their own. That was my premise and was willing to compromise. Show them my culture without feeling ashamed of the primitive media distortions. I wanted to share my cultural dances, story telling, drama, mashairi (poetry) and different dishes. In return I wanted to learn about the American culture, I wanted to know much about the white and black cultures since they made up most of America.

In my quest to explore the other side I had a memorable encounter that tested my ability to cross the great cultural and racial divide. Soon after my two terms as ISO president. I received a phone call from a white girl who was in a sociology class where I had given a talk on dating in our culture. I had not given out my phone number, so I wondered how she got it. But I knew one thing, once you had held a public office; your life was a matter of public knowledge. A phone from a girl on Friday, who could turn it down?

"Can I speak to . . . Aba . . . bio . . . I can't pronounce the name?"

"Ababio is the name." I pretended I was not the one she wanted to reach and took my time answering while pouring a glass of wine. Making sure I was comfortable, I answered the phone.

"Hello."

"Is this Ababio?"

"Speaking."

"Well, I don't think you know me, so I have to introduce myself."

"You have a good voice, go a head."

"I am Melanie and saw you in my sociology class. I liked your speech."

"Really."

"Yeah, I was impressed and want to know more about your customs."

"I'm glad you enjoyed it. What are you doing right now?"

"Nothing really, I was just watching TV with my roommate. Why?"

"Maybe we can meet somewhere for coffee or something?"

"Where?"

"The Tea House. Do you know where that is?"

"Yeah."

"Casual or formal?"

"I don't care what you wear."

"See you there in a little bit."

After we hang up, I took a shower and got ready. After three years in this little town I had gotten used to all kinds of racial stares. There were fears on both sides. My color, since coming to the United States, had become significant. I was thought of as any black guy trying to get lucky. A white seen with me had to fight the stereotypes of being labeled white trash just for trying to befriend a person of color. What the heck, I prepared for the worst. I knew Melanie had a boyfriend, something common to most

American college-aged students. For many foreign students, leaving home at the peak of our youth meant separation and an end of old relationships. So we had time to grow new ones if necessary. With my schedule, though, maintaining a steady relationship with somebody had become very hard. So I tried to keep any friendships less serious since I didn't have much time to invest.

I drove my Datsun to the Tea House and found parking just outside. It was easier for her to spot me since. I had no idea who she was and what she looked like. Sure enough, as soon as I walked in, and she spotted me immediately. All eyes were on me as I was unaccompanied. Most people in the room were white. They looked for a black girl who could be my date, but could not see any. Melanie waved her hand, inviting me to a table reserved for two.

"Ab . . . abio, I'm Melanie."

"Ababio, pleasure to meet you."

"It's my pleasure too."

"Didn't take you long to get here, eh?"

"I just stay in Fitz Hall. What about you?"

"Off campus."

"Off campus, I like the way you say it."

The waitress interrupted us to take our order. "Two teas, please," I ordered.

"So what do people usually do on a Friday evening in Africa?"

"Africa is so big, do you mean Kenya?"

"Ke . . . nia?"

"Friday at home, I would go for a movie or to a club."

"Do they party a lot like we do here?"

"No, they get wasted a lot over here. Back home, people go to college at a later age, like 21 or something."

"Hmm . . . do you plan to go back after completing your education?"

"It is my desire to go back, but it depends on the political situation over there."

"You mentioned that in class, I remember."

"Yes, it is so sad. I have friends who were detained when I left. My former classmate who used to report for *The Nation* was picked up. So, what else about my culture do you want to know?"

"Everything."

"That's a whole lot."

"I'll take notes."

"It will take the whole night to get done."

"I've no other plans for tonight."

"What about your boyfriend?"

"He won't mind."

"Positive?"

I then told her about my culture. Throughout the conversation, she learned a lot of things she had not heard through the media. She thought all Africans marry more than one wife and treat women as personal property. I told her that some Africans in the past, depending on tradition married more than one wife. My uncle was a perfect example. However, I belong to a different generation of Africans. Today post-colonial Africans who believe in monogamy and respect women rights. But I pointed out that I was ashamed of a government like mine that had still very few women in powerful positions. She agreed with me pointing out that even in the United States, there is still a glass ceiling.

"What about race relations?" she asked, as if she had realized I was not completely comfortable with all the guys from the adjacent table eyeing me suspiciously thinking I was trying to hit on a cute-looking blonde.

"That was not a problem until I got here."

"What about South Africa, is it true that blacks kill one another?"

"That is what the media want you to think. Anglo-American conglomerates that control the gold revenue have created that problem. But I don't think apartheid will live forever."

"I admire that freedom fighter in prison."

"Mandela?"

"Yes, Nelson Mandela; he's a brave man."

"Sure, he is."

There was a pause. It was getting close to 9 o'clock and the Teahouse was about to close. I did not know what else she expected. Since she had a boyfriend, going out for a dance was out of question, I thought. But I was wrong. Melanie didn't mind going for a dance. Maybe I would get a chance to ask what she had thought of black people.

The opportunity came as we headed for a pub across Pine Street, a popular Friday nightspot. A lot of people stared at a black man with a white girl. We went to the pub, stayed for a couple of minutes and then left. As we were leaving, I met a buddy of mine, a brother who invited us to a black party downstairs. So, we popped in. Watchful eyes of angry sisters grilled us. Seeing me with a white girl, they did not even say hi. "Africans are sellouts, why do they date white girls, why don't they stick to their own kind. All good brothers just go out with white bitches; he just wants to get some," I overheard somebody lamenting.

"Damn," she cursed again profusely. Melanie felt uncomfortable, intimidated by their stares. What if we were dating for real?

"Wazzup, brother?"

"Nothing much."

"Just, chilling, you know it, my brother," my buddy said, hitting me with a high five. Then he pulled me aside. "Are you with this bitch?"

"She's just a friend."

"Damn sure the bitch looks good. No doubt about it. Good ass. Okay man."

Melanie suddenly felt what it was like to be a minority. The rub music was so loud.

We tried to be comfortable but soon we left and headed home. It once again occurred to me that I was trapped between two conflicting forces. To some blacks on campus, I was a sellout, an Uncle Tom, an imitation white and a collaborator. And to some white people, I was a violent, lazy and unpredictable monster. It was a label one had to live to until proven otherwise. The idea of being held with a reservation. I looked far into the dark night and beyond. To an amorphous world, beyond race . . . then to the woman beside me.

"Can we do this again?" I asked trying to brush off the embarrassment.

"Sure."

Taking a leaf from this past encounter, I have come to the realization that as an African and black man, I have to struggle and ignore all forms of stereotypes. I have come to the realization that there are bad apples in any society. There are Africans who have refused to shed part of their culture and assimilate into the American culture. There are Africans who have refused to reach out and meet America halfway. To most of these, America might react with the same cold feet. These might see themselves as victims of race. Some might argue that if America was bad, most immigrants will have no reason to sacrifice to reach her shores. It might be fit to conclude that for one to succeed in this country of immigrants, we might have to break away from our national heritage and try to assimilate into some one culture that is American. Doing that might make us strangers to our past intact cultures, it might drive us from the idea of being victims whenever possible. Similarly, it might be of help if as Africans fighting against all odds we can achieve the respect and harvest the fruits of hard labor and honest toil without being captivated by some stereotypes from the past.

16

BEYOND A TRIBE, BEYOND A RACE

We are born to a particular tribe or race. I was born into a Kisii tribe in Kenya, and then moved on to break away from the shackles of tribe, from the shackles of national boundary; from the shackles of culture; away from the continent. I had to move away in search of opportunity, beyond my tribe, beyond my race. Along the road, I had to shed some parts of me and gain some new ways, some of them at a pretty high cost.

Kenya is a land where all races shake hands, black, white, Asian and Arab. In this land, down below the hills, where I was born, I've grown up seeing different traditions and beliefs. I have grown to see hate of one tribe by another. I have witnessed what strict traditions can breed such as dating along tribal or cultural lines.

Human beings are all the same. Our environment shapes us.

When a child is born, he or she has to learn to adapt to the environment. For example, a Kisii boy in the country learns the Kisii language as that is the closest at hand and then he later learns, other languages. In the same way, a Kisii boy born in an urban area will learn Swahili first, and then Kisii as a second language. This is because, people employ house maids who take care of the young ones from diverse tribes and Swahili is the only language that brings them together, or rather it is the language that transcends tribal boundaries. It is the fabric that knits us together.

Like most Kenyans, I had to leave my tribal birthplace after primary education when I moved to an urban area to start my secondary education. It was a tender age to be transplanted. So, in terms of reaching out for friends, I had to look beyond my tribe. I had to break out of those tribal shells at an early age. In so doing, I realized how important a tribeless Kenya would be, a place where each of us could be a Kenyan first and a tribe member second. In reaching out, I became a different person.

In dating, I have also tried to reach out beyond my tribe and race. This is not in contempt for a woman of my own tribe or race; it is not in contempt for a woman of my own national origin; nor is it an attempt to run away from my tribe, national origin or race. It is an attempt to look at the totality of the individual. I know what this entails. It involves risks. It means walking away. It is a punch in the face of tribalists, nationalists, religious fanatics, racists and bigots.

As a young person I realize that in any society, certain traditions are kept. I went to school in a mixed urban area where all cultures mingled freely. Whether Muslim, Hindu or Christian, there was a common bond. However, older people maintained the strict cultural barriers, which I swore to tear to shreds.

Cultures, for whatever reason, have created their own form of homelands; some form of cultural apartheids. For example, some cultures do not allow intercultural dating. It was not easy for non- Muslim to date a Moslem, or an Asian to date an African. An African dating a white was still regarded with so much curiosity.

"Will she speak my language?" my mother asked me one day learning of my desire one day to go to America, a white country, and possibly marry a white woman.

"She'll learn," I replied.

"Really, will she learn our language and culture?"

"Ndio mama, atafundishwa"(Yes mom she will learn), I answered.

I knew, though, that my mother would open-heartedly embrace anyone I brought home whether a Muslim, Asian, white or anyone from the 48 tribes in Kenya. Her question involved her ability to communicate with her.

My desire to free myself from this cultural and traditional apartheid increased even more when I left the country and came to the States where the appetite for variety is insatiable. For any country to grow, some cultural barriers must be broken. For an independent and free Kenya to come to fruition, people must be able to break out of those shackles of culture.

As I spent time in the United States, I became more than willing to cross the cultural divide. I knew that to learn something new, sacrifices were necessary. Initially, I was afraid that in trying to embrace a new culture, I was losing some of my roots. So it was a tough balancing act. While at Central Missouri State University, I faced tough challenges in trying to lead a student organization whose composition included Islamic students from the Middle East and Pakistan, Jewish students from Israel as well as American students. Islamic students abhorred absolute beliefs emanating from the tensions in their homeland. The Palestinian-Israel conflict was a delicate powder keg. It was on one of these occasions that a student from Tel Aviv admitted to me the magnitude of the conflict.

"I'm willing to have a booth at the festival, but I am afraid."

"Why are you afraid," I asked.

"The Arab students will boycott the whole exhibit."

"But this is a university exhibit."

"I know but . . ." She could not continue.

"I looked at her willingness to do the impossible, then felt helpless like an infant. Some Muslim students were planning to boycott the whole show. I felt she was a victim of tensions that have divided her homeland for years. Some of these were so deep-rooted that they could not go away in a day.

"I understand," I said trying to imagine myself in her situation. I knew that all these ancient feuds could not be solved in a day but we must start somewhere. Our student organization was best suited to carry on that mission.

Incidents such as this helped intensify my resolve to loosen my self and bring forces of division to their knees. I had come to America to make use of an opportunity. America is the only place that has given me a chance to break away from old cultural walls and traditions without feeling any remorse. Although walking away from deep cultural roots and traditions had its cost, I was determined to be part of a new community in a New World where religion, race or cultural origin played no part. Although we could feed off the strengths of the origins of such cultures, I wanted to be part of an organization where diversity was necessary as a source from which we could derive our strength.

I am determined to be a man in the New World, an individual against society. I am determined to derive from my traditions and culture the best that will enable me thrive in this new environment without being a stranger or being captive. This is the kind of life that I'm striving to live. It is the life of an individual. My life.

17

CHANCES ARE

I came to America at the pinnacle of my youth. At just 21, the experience of separating from my family was not easy. I was away from home for so long that distance and separation totally changed my relationship with my childhood friends. So I had to make new friends. Like a traveler, I had no claim on a permanent base. I had to adjust to new surroundings, making friends out of strangers.

My first hardship was in language. Coming from a former British colony, my English was a mixture of British English and my native language. I had trouble distinguishing my pronunciation of the words "live" and "leave" and "mud" and "mad," "sheep and ship" While I tried hard to get these words correct, some people were impatient when trying to understand me, which made learning American English difficult. Sometimes, when I asked for something in the cafeteria, the server would be so impatient and I would end up pointing to a particular food item. Seeing me do so, some students would laugh loud at my inconvenience. One day while I was standing on the food line, I tried to let the server know what dish I wanted by snapping my fingers. I was devastated when she retorted, "Don't do that, I am not a dog." Such was the change in mannerisms that frustrated me as I struggled to settle in the new land. I tried so hard to learn American English and at the same time, I started losing the accuracy and proper usage of the English language. Curse words that I had hitherto used sparingly were now routine. Instead of "goodness" or "Goodness gracious," it was "damn," in place of "bloody," it was "holy shit." Whereas at home one could be in trouble for breaking rules of the English language, in America people got away with what I thought was a complete massacre of the language. Thus, to learn and adjust, I wrestled with the new language. As part of that, I tried to be patient with Americans who I thought talked very fast. But nobody seemed to be particularly helpful. But I got a consolation from the way they butchered my name.

My second obstacle with language was the usage of certain words. In my native country, the words, "sweetheart," "honey" and "darling" were used on special occasions, like when addressing your lover or someone with whom you are romantically involved. In America, as I came to find out, these words were used loosely, making me feel very uncomfortable. One time a cook in the cafeteria called me "sweetheart" while asking me to wipe some table. I became so nervous thinking she was making a pass at me that I did not know how to respond since she was my mom's age. On another occasion, a female in my math class used the word "honey" when referring to me. Having been used to thinking that the word was used only to address someone for whom I one had romantic feelings, I thought she had a crush on me. Wrong! As I learned when I tried to ask her out and learned that she had a boyfriend.

No matter how I tried to adjust as time went by, I realized that I had to stick to my mixture of British English and my native tongue, even though it meant speaking with an accent and as a way of maintaining my identity. The more I kept my language, the more comfortable I felt the better I stood my ground. As long as my writing skills were better than those of my detractors, I felt no remorse. I was vindicated when my essays and speeches scored high grades and were read in front of class. One time my communication skills instructor asked me if she could keep a copy of my paper to show her next semester students, to which I obliged.

The third obstacle in settling as a student in an American university was juggling work and studies. In my native country, there is no continuous assessment. At the beginning of the semester, students are given a syllabus listing topics of importance and at the end of the term, they sit for a comprehensive exam. If you flunk, you're doomed. However, you have the whole semester to prepare. Besides, since most students don't work there are no jobs anyway, they study harder, spending the day in class and going to the library at night.

Also, at home, we used to have debates and open forums where students exchanged ideas, but in American University settings, students are so busy juggling work and classes that they don't have time and often remain strangers on campus.

Testing itself posed a problem, since many exams were multiple-choice. Whereas most American students loved them, I hated multiple-choice type of questions because I was used to essay questions. As a result, I struggled and one time got 70%. At home that mark would be hard to achieve, as the exams were essay in nature, detailed and comprehensive. My grade was a C. Unsatisfied, I went to the teacher and asked for an essay exam. I got 96%. I still thank the professor for giving me an option. And yet, for those who have not got this option and fail to pass at the beginning, I feel the system has room for improvement. Not that the system is bad. It still has a lot of good but has room for improvement.

Lack of thoroughness and reading between the lines got me in trouble one day. I went to the housing department and signed a residence contract not knowing that there was no exit clause. Once one signed, one had to stay in the dorm for a full year before moving out. Although I was 21 years old and eligible for off-campus housing, I was forced to stay in the residence hall at double the price an American student paid. Without a job on campus, I became financially strapped. As a foreigner to a new environment, I was ignorant of the laws that, if read clearly to me ahead of time, could have made a difference.

As the days went by, I was introduced to spending extravagantly and living for the moment. When one time the heel on my shoe needed to be replaced, I was told to get a whole new pair of shoes. When my pant zipper needed a minor repair, I was told to replace it. At home, such repairs could be done cheaply. In this aspect, I felt America was very wasteful.

With time, I have come to realize that the initial challenges only made me strong. They hardened my resolve and desire to work hard in order to fulfill the American dream. In any society, nothing good comes easier. However the challenges, chances are that with hard work, American offers an opportunity. However bumpy the road might be, chances are that America can graft the best from an individual. However indifferent racial groups can be toward others in this melting pot, chances are that America has the potential to be the greatest country on the face of the earth.

18

THE BONDS THAT BIND US

Coming to America, I had dreams of learning from black America of their struggles and past experiences. In return, I expected to tell them about my home, my culture the real Africa, not the media creation. The dances and joys of the continent as told by people who live it. I wanted to tell them about my family, the dreams of welcoming them home for a visit. While on the road, it has been sad to watch these dreams crumble in front of me. How- ever, I have met friends, the likes of Phil, Ken and the few who have expressed a desire to visit my country one day and see for themselves the real Africa. Let's start with Pete, a Yellow Cab driver, whom I met one day when I took my car to the garage for service and to get back home I called a taxi. I had developed this idea of talking to older black folks about the state of black America. He too wanted to know why Africans come here to America and manage to make inroads where black Americans have not.

"How come Africans, Chinese, Mexicans, Jamaicans come here and make it while most black young men do not?" he asked looking at a young black man on the side of the street holding a bottle of colt45 wrapped partially in a paper bag. He opened the conversation with this question.

"Where are you from, Jamaica?"

"No, I am from Kenya,"

"Mm. How long have you been here?"

"Almost 12 years."

"Are you going back?"

"I will some day, but things are not good there right now."

"What do you do, go to school?"

"I am done with school; I am a chemist by profession."

"Good, good for you." Pause . . . "I wish most black people from here would pursue professions like that. You see, it is very hard at my age to go to school. I had no opportunity during time. I am 50 years old but I tell my sons that they have all the opportunities, loans, an affirmative action and all sorts of minority programs. Instead of dreaming of playing sports, I wish most of them thought like you folks from the outside. It is so hard getting any business in the black neighborhood. Look at me, my shirt cost $15.00, my pants $25.00, and my boots $35.00 at Payless. Now do I look like a rich man you?"

"No."

"When I drive this taxi cab, people think I am rich and they want to rob me. Sometimes, when I drop off somebody and tell them the fare is $6.00, their comment is, "Six dollars? That is expensive, I could've taken a bus.""

"It is so hard to deal with your own people and it hurts so much. Most people blame racism for everything, but we have to move past that. As for me, I plan to buy mowing equipment and seek some contracts to mow lawns in your side of town. I tell my kids go to school, that way you won't blame the system for not giving you a job. You cannot get a good job without education. Once you're turned down, you start blaming 'em white folks. It is not always true."

There was some silence. Then I told him, "I have seen that all my life. I come from a black country and see that all the time. I have been through college and still the issue is the same. We are good at blaming everything on racism and yet blacks themselves go at each other every day.

Whenever one wants to succeeded, the rest tend to pull them down."

"I wish most black folks thought like you." Pause. "Do I turn right here?"

"Yes, then right at the stoplight."

Whenever we shake hands, the conversation is both casual and non-committal.

It never goes beyond simply "What is up brother". We never go beyond issues such as where you come from, as is usually the case with any other group of people. We live in different areas of town, some of us on the other side.

Sometimes sandwiched between both. A classic example can be illustrated by this brief encounter at a suburban pub.

I walked into a pub one evening after along day's work. Being in the suburb, it was frequented by generally a white crowd. I, infact, was the only black soul that night. I have grown used to this after all the years on the road. So I walked in fearlessly and took my seat at the counter. Soon after I had ordered a drink, the person sitting one seat way from me snuggled closer and wanted to engage me in a conversation. It was obvious that I was black and alone, so he wanted to make me feel comfortable.

"Hey man, how are you doing?"

"Fine."

"You've got an accent, where are you from?"

"Kenya."

"Mm . . . Must be damned! I knew you were not from here. Well, where is that around, Cape Carde?"

"No, it is in East Africa, right by the Indian Ocean."

He then spoke in a lifeless, eerie tone. "You know, man, this shit about black and white. I don't understand it."

"I know. It is the way of life."

At the same time he gestured the waitress, offering to buy me a drink. I accepted knowing that I was going to return a round.

"Bud light for me, what about you?"

"A glass of wine will do."

"Nice ass she got there," he commented as an aside referring to the cocktail waitress.

As the waitress left to get the drinks, another black person entered the bar making the number of blacks in the room two. He looked to have spent a great deal of time in the gym. My new white friend recognized him and proceeded to introduce us, "Hey, Darrell, meet my fella here from Africa."

"Yea, that's cool." Darrell shook his head and took his seat next to me. He ordered a drink with his eyes glued to the bartender. Soon she brought our orders and received her tip.

It was my white friend's idea to keep us talking, expecting presumably that Darrell would ask more about Africa. But he was wrong thinking that it was easy for an African and a black American to talk about Africa. Darrell sipped his broth, a Heineken import and kept eyeing the bartender. We did not have anything in common apart from the fact that we were both black. Darrell looked at his white buddy; he looked at me and to the bartender, and yet said nothing. Here we were once again in a state of suspicion. We had nothing in common as it looked on the surface. And that remains a mirror of society. A black man is the same. It is hard to get a chance to distinguish yourself from the common stereotypes. This mum state has and still to most of us remains a complete mystery.

Is there any hope for any relationship between Africans and Black America? If you asked me the answer to this question, I don't know. What I know is that there remains a lot of potential. Black Americans by virtue of having their ancestors in Africa have the responsibility of tracing their roots to that continent. This can be in form of taking trips to Africa, learning about the culture and establishing closer ties. They can also play a greater role in promoting democratic principles in Africa. Whenever stubborn African dictators hear anything from white leaders, they claim racism. If they hear the criticism from Black leaders, it will be very hard to hide behind the same bias.

On this road I am traveling, I have met people from all persuasions. I have met and continue to meet black people who want me to tell them and their children about my home. I have met good and bad black people. I hope to meet those who will welcome not only me to their homes but other Africans who still have to live with all this burden of trying to prove that they are not imitation whites. My hope is that one day, black America will do to Africa what the Jewish community has done to Israel. When that day comes, I and other African immigrants will feel proud of having a friendly big brother and not an adversary. I and other African immigrants will have a reason to be proud for we will become one. We will reconnect the umbilical cords snapped by years of separation from the continent knowing the fact that we encounter the same challenges and tribulations. And these are the bonds that bind us.

19

WHERE MY COUNTRY FELL SHORT WITH ME

I will write what I want,
Now that I am away from your spies
In mad pursuit to silence
All conduits of truth And so validate your rule
Of fear and silence... Ababio.86

left home at 21 and came to America in search of an opportunity. I believed that America had immense opportunities to offer any immigrant who came across her shores. I believed that America offered freedom to express divergent points of view. I left my country, family and friends because my young country lacked opportunities for me. The country of my birth could not provide opportunities for an emerging young population. I left at a time when tensions had risen to new heights. I watched with dismay as political leaders barricaded themselves in the state houses. I watched helplessly as my country ruled by the newly propertied class squashed any form of opposition. I watched helplessly as some friends who were journalists were detained without trial. Under these circumstances, I helplessly gave up my dream of utilizing my God given potential to the full, to be a journalist, a career that became very risky. So one morning in the summer of 1986, I left but with a desire to return someday.

I came to America to equip myself with enough knowledge to enable me to compete on the world stage. Since I was born after independence, I wanted to gain enough knowledge to enable me play a role in an independent Kenya. Growing up our leaders always emphasized that the future of the country depended on the young people. However, I was wrong. Once corrupted by absolute power, leaders were willing to leave by bullet instead of ballot. As the days went by, my country sunk into a pot of tribalism fanned by leaders who sat pitting one tribe against another. The country had been turned into a police state with roadblocks everywhere. If you are not well connected to the ruling party, you have no place in that country. It is ironic that independence meant freeing ourselves from colonial leaders only to be enslaved by our own people. We had not moved out of jail but been merely moved into another form of imprisonment.

Now, almost fourteen years after leaving the country, I still don't see much chance of affecting any changes there. It is hard to make any change from outside. I am much a stranger to what is happening in that country. It can be argued by those who have experienced the brutality of the system that people like us can criticize the system because we have ran away. We have escaped the watchful eyes of Moi's police state. It is hard to disagree with them. You see what is wrong with your country when you are outside. Whereas Moi measures Kenya's progress in comparison to warton neighboring countries like Somalia and Sudan, we compare ourselves against developed countries.

In this road that has come to be my home, sometimes I come across Kenyans who have decided to settle down in our new adopted home. Sometimes we spend a lot of hours arguing on how our native country fell short with us. Strangely, with time, it is hard to see the country of my boyhood days. Once transplanted from the native culture, time can erase bonds. One becomes impatient at the rate at which things are done. The cultures start clashing and one becomes a stranger to his own native land. It becomes hard to accept the validity of previously accepted traditional values. One tends to overcome habits, behavior and shortcomings that plague our native country. One tends to move away from the selfishness of culture and tribal differences in an effort to mould an amorphous Kenyan communit y. S ometimes there's some success and sometimes the alternative occurs resulting in little colonies where the native cultural and tribal feuds stripe themselves naked.

In the case of Ramji, an Indian and fellow Kenyan from Parklands, a dominantly Indian suburb in Nairobi, strict Indian culture and uncertainty about Kenya's future have contributed to his desire to settle and pledge his allegiance to his newly adopted land. Ramji like most of us was born in Kenya after independence. His parents emigrated originally from India. In high school he went by his nickname "chute". Recently, I met Ramji, who was unemployed at the time. We started talking about Kenya. We talked about Kenya of our boyhood days and the changes that have taken place. What follows is part of the conversation.

Ababio: "So why aren't you going back, I thought you guys own almost everything in the country?

Ramji: "I like it here man, hapa fiti, hakuna wasiwasi."

Ababio: "Kweli."

Ramji: "Indian culture is very closed man that as much as I want to be free I find myself in chains. My parents have predetermined my future for me. They expect me to be this and that. They'll feel proud bragging to their friends, that my son in America is coming back to marry some rich Indian's daughter. I don't feel the same. When I was in Kenya, I wanted to date someone outside my culture, but it was taboo. So man, here I have found my chance and it is different. I feel at peace with myself. Whether they accept it or not, I don't give a shit."

Ababio: "Is your wife Kenyan or America?"

Ramji: "Mkikuyu bwana."

Ababio: "Mmm . . . it is very rare to find that in your culture. What's is her name?"

Ramji: "Ciiru."

Ababio: "Any kids?"

Ramji: "Kijana mmoja, Toto, see how cute the little boy is." Ababio: "Very cute, Pongezi bwana! (Congrats). I admire people like you man. I know how hard it is sometimes." There was a pause.

Ramji: "So man, that is why I have decided to be an American and live here. That way we can raise our son to appreciate both cultures."

Ababio: "That is smart, very smart thing to do."

Ramji: "Na wewe, umeoa mzungu ama? (Are you married to an American)."

Ababio: "Mimi sipague, ikiwa mzungu ama mwafrika bora tusikizane (I don't care whether it is an American or African as long as we can get along)."

Ramji: "Wasi."

Ababio: "Do you meet other Kenyans?"

Ramji: "Lakini hata hapa bwana. Mimi na hawa wakenya wenzangu, hawanijulishi linalotendeka. Najikia wakati mwingine kama mtawa" (even us Kenyans, I feel like an outsider within my own community. No one lets me know what is happening. I feel like a hermit sometimes).

Ababio: "It is a total reflection of our country. The evils of tribalism still manifest within us. That is why I have decided against staying in a little colony of Kenyans where you eat the same food, talk the same language, fight over the same pool of women, and witness the same tribal and cultural feuds we ran away from. It is hard to learn anything new.

It is sad, how people from one country can coin in one struggle.
Whereby my country has fallen short with me by not providing opportunity, your culture has fallen short with you by not accepting your

choices. It is a travesty, such a betrayal that one has to be forced to find a place to belong."

It could be argued that Kenya as a country is not responsible for alleviating all of Ramji's fears. It is the responsibility of the Indian culture to open up and make it easier for people of different desires and needs to thrive. However, it is the responsibility of the government to ensure that conditions exist for all groups to coexist without fear or retribution. It is the responsibility of the government to ensure that all groups that make up Kenya have an equal chance of relishing the fruits of independence.

Such a spirit can then spread from the country to the foreign lands where Kenyan nationals might inhabit. Until then, the dream of Kenyans as a country will be an aborted dream. We must desist from seeing ourselves in terms of tribe, subculture or religious group to Kenyans first. Kenyans who shall be coined in language and hopes for the betterment of that country.

Is there any hope for Kenya? One might ask. The future of that country does not depend on politicians who have otherwise prostituted it. It does not depend on intellectuals who have turned into political choirboys. The future of that country depends on ordinary people. It depends on the ability of these people to reach out irrespective of which tribe or culture they emanate from. It will take the likes of little Toto, Ramji's, Ciiru's, Oles, Barasas and Alis. It is my hope then that the face of a new Kenya will come out of this mould, where tribe, race or cultural boundaries will be a thing, of the past. Where the culture of cronyism, nepotism and corruption will be a thing of the past. When that day comes, I will say oh Kenya, you've not fallen short with me, oh Kenya you've made me proud.

20

AND YET I KEEP
ON WALKING

"The United States offers, as does no other nation, a limit- less opportunity: here a man can go as far his abilities will carry him or *her*. It may be that the foreign born, as in my case must hold on to some ideals and ideals of the land of his birth; it may be that he or *her* must develop and mould his or *her* character by overcoming the habits resulting from national shortcomings.

But into the best that the foreign-born can retain, America can graft such a wealth of inspiration, so high a national idealism, and so great an opportunity for the highest en- deavor, as to make him or *her* the fortunate man or *woman* of the earth to day."

Edward Bok. (*Italics mine*)

For a long time, I waited and hoped things would get better only to find that the situation had gotten worse. I had hoped education would help and bridge the divide. But this has merely turned into a pipe dream. In some instances, we have only scorched the snake of tribalism but not burnt it. We should strive and take risks even though this might take casualties.

Perhaps someday people will be free from those same cultural apartheids and run to a place where they can be part of the soup in the melting pot. Perhaps people will some day walk past the racial divides and bring down those walls of indifference. Perhaps an African will walk beyond the sleeping continent and shake hands amicably with black or white Americans, Chinese or Asian. Perhaps a Kenyan will walk beyond tribal or ethnic boundaries.

If in life we stumble, we need to lift ourselves and rise again. Sometimes, as foreigners, we have no control of our destiny. We cannot decide when to settle down because sometimes each day is a struggle. But the challenges we face only harden our resolve and desire to succeed. I have tried to use my stumbles on the way to fight harder and avoid being a victim of my race even though I am reminded of race each and every day whether in banks or mortgage applications. In one way or another we encounter it. I have tried to treat any failure as only a failure; that and not as a result of my color or my race.

America might have her problems in terms of race relations, but she still remains a place that offers opportunity to succeed. Despite the challenges, I am thankful to the American people. I thank America for the opportunity to allow me pursue the elusive American dream.

Notes:

1. Whitman, Walt. *Leaves of Grass* (New York: Vintage books, Division of Random House, Inc., 1992), p. 302.
2. Wathiongo, Ngugi. *Homecoming* (Lawrence Hill &Company Publishers Inc., 1973), p. 42
3. Wathiongo, Ngugi: *Homecoming* (Lawrence Hill & Company Publishers Inc., 1973), p. 23
4. Hunter, Gordon. *Immigrant Voices* (New York: Penguin Inc., 1999), p. 210.